Grandma, I don't want to go to sleep

A Forever Love Tale

D1089371

For the grandmothers who sacrificed
Who played the role of mother twice.
Be it a little girl or little boy
You filled their tiny lives with joy.
- RC -

For the grandmothers
who are always at our side.
- TM -

Grandma, I don't want to go to sleep

A Forever Love Tale

By

Richard Ceasor

Illustrations by

Thelma Muraida

CEASOR PRESS PUBLISHING

Grandma, I don't want to go to sleep!

I want to dive below the gentle waves
of an ocean dark and deep.

We all need to sleep,
it won't seem that long.
You must get your sleep,
to grow up tall and strong.

But I don't want to go to sleep.

I want to push an octopus,
or tickle a dolphin's fin.
And each time we get together
do it all again.

We all need to sleep
I don't have to tell you why.
It's the only way that you can go
to the land where children fly.

But I don't want to go to sleep.

I want to make a wish with a fish
it's his birthday you see.

Or share a tale with a whale
as he has some fun with me.

"I don't want to sleep!" I said.

But still the pillow found my head.
And as I slowly closed my eyes
grandma said her last goodbye.

About the Author

From Martial Arts master inducted in the Martial Arts Hall of Fame, to a singer who has sang on the stage as a member of The Platters, to a corporate outside sales representative who left corporate America to go teach inner-city children in Washington DC. Richard Ceasor brings a wealth of experience to his writing.

Richard has taught children for almost two decades in inner city and Title I schools. He has also worked as a District Wide Behavior Specialist and a Disciplinary Alternative Education Program Principal and has spent many hours with both troubled and non troubled young people.

About the Illustrator

Thelma Muraida is an accomplished artist and designer from San Antonio, Texas. She has illustrated five picture books, seven early childhood readers and has contibuted to several early childhood curriculum materials and nonprofit agencies. Thelma has also exhibited her artwork nationally.

From an early age, Thelma was inspired by the intense colors and textures of her cultural surroundings. In her use of color and form she explores the balance that can come with memory and emotion making connections to tell a visual story whether as a storybook or a finished work of art.

Introduction

Heavy artillery in the calibres between 106 and 210 mm covers a range from field pieces to massive siege pieces intended for firing against static emplacements. At the lower end of the scale and up to about 155 mm most of the pieces mentioned in this Fact File formed the main striking power of most of the artillery formations used during World War 2. Most Continental armies defined their heavy artillery as starting with 105 mm guns and these have been mentioned in a previous Fact File but the bulk of the heavy field artillery rested with 150 and 155 mm guns and howitzers. The guns were used to provide a direct and heavy supporting fire and were also used for long-range interdiction in rear and supply areas, while the howitzers were more often used to provide a heavy plunging fire against battlefield targets. Above 155 mm most heavy pieces were used in relatively static warfare as their great weight and bulk made them difficult to move quickly and easily. Exceptions were the German 17 cm and 21 cm pieces and the Italian 210 mm field howitzer.

A quick search through this File will soon reveal that a large number of the gun and howitzers mentioned had their origins before and during World War 1. The conditions of that conflict dictated the use of large numbers of heavy pieces and left most of the combatants with large stocks of heavy artillery. The high cost of replacing the masses of still serviceable artillery was beyond the purses of all but the very richest nations between the wars and as a result the artillery parks of most nations in 1939 were little different from those of 1918. However, most nations had contrived to make the existing pieces into viable weapons by modernising the projectiles fired with improvements both in range and destructive powers, and by improving their mobility. Pieces that were horsedrawn in 1918 were by 1939 often drawn by modern tractors, and large weapons that were once broken down into loads in order to keep their bulk under control were by 1939 often towed in one load. This reduced the time in and out of action but often involved the use of trail limbers that added to the travelling weight. But it must be emphasised that in 1939 many heavy field pieces were towed into action in a manner little different from that of 1918.

Despite the financial difficulties of the years between the wars much work had gone into research and development of new field pieces and although many promising designs had to be shelved, in 1939 there were some new types in service in Europe. Germany in particular was equipped with a whole new range of guns and howitzers but experience in battle, particularly in Russia, revealed that many of the German designs lacked range and striking power. In some ways the German re-armament campaign began too early for the late 1930s saw a whole new range of metallurgical and chemical discoveries that advanced the gunner's art a great deal in a very short time. Many of these discoveries came too late for the German programme but were applied to the re-armament programmes of Russia, the UK and the USA. Thus by 1942 the Germans frequently found themselves outranged by foreign artillery and despite frantic improvement programmes had to equip their artillery units with amounts of captured artillery until their own superior designs could be produced. This is not to say that all German heavy artillery was of little use. Their 17 cm K 18 and 21 cm Mrs 18 were superb weapons, but many of their 15 cm equipments did not match up to their requirements in battle and were kept in production only because there was nothing on hand to replace them.

The Russians were in the process of replacing their heavy artillery when the Germans invaded in 1941. A refurbishing programme had been started on the many antiquated pieces in use with the Red Army during the early 1930s but in 1941 there were still many elderly unmodified pieces in service. During 1941 many of these old weapons were either captured or destroyed and at the same time much of the Russian manufacturing plant came under German occupation. As a result the Russians had to turn out large numbers of weapons and they virtually standardised on only two calibres—122 and 152 mm. These two calibres made up the bulk of the Russian artillery output and the standardisation of calibres made the production of standard projectiles relatively easy and as a result the supply situation was made much easier in the field than it could ever have been for many other armies. The Russian heavy artillery was on the whole a formidable and fearsome weapon of war. The guns and howitzers used were sound rugged pieces and by 1944 they were available in huge numbers.

The situation in the UK and USA was very like that of the USSR in 1939. Delays and lack of funds had prevented re-equipment until the very last moment

but after 1940 both nations were well on the way to providing new weapons for the heavy artillery units. In France and Italy the situation was different. Both nations were left with masses of heavy artillery after 1918 and between the wars little could be done to replace it. As a result France went to war with World War 1 weapons in 1939 and lost the lot in 1940. In a way, the Italians were even worse off than the French for they lacked the industrial base to manufacture large numbers of new artillery pieces. They made some efforts during the late 1930s to replace their antique artillery but they never managed to produce enough to even start to replace the backlog of obsolete equipment. They produced a number of very good designs but never in quantity. The situation in Japan was very similar to that of Italy.

The weapons described in this Fact File formed the main bulk of the many massive barrages of World War 2. As such they must be held responsible for the destruction of towns and cities and for the loss of life and injury caused to civilian and soldier alike. Heavy artillery has had this responsibility for centuries and even now, in 1975, the advent of the aircraft and guided missile has not dislodged it from its position as 'the last argument of Kings'.

Photo Credits
Bruno Benvenuti
Major R. A. Riccio
Franz Kosar
Imperial War Museum
Bundesarchiv
E.C.A. (France)
S M E-Ufficio Storico (Italy)

BELGIUM

Canon de 120 L mle 1931

Produced by the Société anonyme John Cockerill, the mle 1931 began to enter Belgian Army service in 1934 and in 1939 there were 24 in use. The mle 1931 was a rather heavy weapon with a large split trail carriage held down in action by large trail spades pushed down into the ground. It had a good range and fired a most useful shell but its values were also appreciated by the Germans and after 1940 the mle 1931 continued in use as the 12 cm K 370(b).

DATA
CALIBRE   120 mm   4.72 in
LENGTH OF PIECE (L/37)   4426 mm
   174.25 in
LENGTH OF RIFLING   3562 mm   140.23 in
WEIGHT TRAVELLING   5800 kg   12,789 lb
WEIGHT IN ACTION   5450 kg   12,017 lb
ELEVATION   0° to 38° 30′
TRAVERSE   60°
M.V.   760 m/s   2494 ft/sec
MAXIMUM RANGE   17,500 m   19,145 yards
SHELL WEIGHT   21.93 kg   48.355 lb

Canon de 155 L mle 1924

This gun was one of the largest pieces ever produced by the Belgian Cockerill arsenal to actually see service and it began its service career in the late 1920s. It was a conventional gun which was transported in two parts and was designed from the start for mechanical traction. The exact number of these guns in Belgian service is not recorded but was probably not more than 24. After 1940 these guns were taken into the German fold as the 15.5 cm K 432(b).

DATA
CALIBRE   155 mm   6.1 in
LENGTH OF PIECE (L/30.48)   4721 mm
   185.86 in
LENGTH OF RIFLING   3280.5 mm   129.15 in
WEIGHT TRAVELLING (complete)   8900 kg
   19,625 lb
WEIGHT IN ACTION   7840 kg   17,287 lb
ELEVATION   +5° to 26°
TRAVERSE   4°
M.V.   665 m/s   2182 ft/sec
MAXIMUM RANGE   17,000 m   18,600 yards
SHELL WEIGHT   43 kg   94.8 lb

CZECHOSLOVAKIA

Skoda 149 mm Model 14

DATA (Obice da 149/12)
CALIBRE   149.1 mm   5.87 in
LENGTH OF PIECE (L/14)   2090 mm
   82.29 in
LENGTH OF BARREL   1806 mm   71.11 in
LENGTH OF RIFLING (L/11)   1644.5 mm
   64.75 in
WEIGHT TRAVELLING   3070 kg   6769 lb
WEIGHT IN ACTION   2344 kg   5168 lb
ELEVATION   —5° to 43°
TRAVERSE   5°
M.V.   300 m/s   984 ft/sec
MAXIMUM RANGE   6900 m   7550 yards
SHELL WEIGHT   41 kg   90.4 lb

1. *Obice da 149/12 modello 16-18* 2. *Obice da 149/12 modello 14* 3. *Obice da 149/12 modello 16-18. This was an Italian modification of the basic Skoda design* 4. *Obice da 149/12 in action*

The Skoda M.14 was one of the more important pieces in use by the Austria-Hungarian army during World War 1 and after 1918 it was kept in use by the new Czech, Austrian and Hungarian armies. It was soon withdrawn from use by the Czechs but remained in use in Austria until 1938 when the type was taken into the Wehrmacht inventory as the 15 cm sFH M.14 (Skoda). These howitzers were kept in use (some were fitted with muzzle brakes) as 'standard' field pieces until at least 1943 on the Russian Front. The Hungarian guns were also still in use in 1939 but these guns had been updated by the Hungarian MAVAG concern to produce the M.14/35, and a later development was the M.14/39M—not much is known about these pieces. In 1918 the Italians had captured enough M.14 howitzers from the Austro-Hungarian army to take the type into their own inventory and the M.14 then became the Obice da 149/12 modello 14. In this form it was used widely during World War 2 (in 1939 the Italians had 490 on hand) and eventually came under German control in 1943 as the 15 cm sFH 400(i). The M.14 was a conventional and sturdy piece which gave its many users good service.

1

2

3

4

Skoda 149 mm Model 14/16

The Skoda M.14/16 was a 1916 progressive improvement on the basic M.14. It differed in changes to the barrel and featured a strengthened carriage. The type became one of the mainstays of the new Czech army in 1919 and was used as the 15 cm hrubá houfnice vz. 14/16 but by 1938 it had been withdrawn from use. During World War 1 the Italians had captured sufficient to equip their army with the M.14/16 as a 'standard' weapon and to them it was known as the Obice da 149/13. It was used during most of the campaigns in which the Italian army was involved during the period from 1940 to 1943 and many pieces were fitted with new wheels and redesigned shields to modernise the design. After the Italian surrender in 1943 many of these elderly howitzers were taken over as the 15 cm sFH 401(i) by German forces in Italy.

DATA (Obice da 149/13)
CALIBRE   149.1 mm   5.87 in
LENGTH OF PIECE (L/14.1)   2100 mm   82.69 in
LENGTH OF BARREL   1835.6 mm   72.27 in
LENGTH OF RIFLING (L/10.3)   1542.1 mm   60.72 in
WEIGHT TRAVELLING   3340 kg   7365 lb
WEIGHT IN ACTION   2765 kg   6097 lb
ELEVATION   —5° to 70°
TRAVERSE   6°
M.V. (max)   350 m/s   1148 ft/sec
MAXIMUM RANGE   8790 m   9616 yards
SHELL WEIGHT   40.33 kg   88.9 lb

*1. 15 cm hrubá houfnice vz. 14/16 **2,4.** Obice da 149/13 **3.** This Obice da 149/13 in Africa shows the latest version with a re-designed shield and wheels*

1

2

3

4

Skoda 149 mm Model 15

DATA
CALIBRE 149.1 mm 5.87 in
LENGTH OF PIECE (L/20) 2990 mm 117 in
WEIGHT IN ACTION 5560 kg 12,260 lb
ELEVATION —5° to 65°
TRAVERSE 8°
M.V. 508 m/s 1667 ft/sec
MAXIMUM RANGE 11,500 m 12,580 yards
SHELL WEIGHT 42 kg 92.6 lb

The Skoda M.15 was derived from a fortification howitzer and was unusual in being designed for towing in one load behind a petrol-driven vehicle—in 1915 most pieces were still being designed for horse traction. The M.15 was intended for use along the border between Austria and Italy and as this region was mountainous the piece could be broken down into four loads. Only 57 were built and after 1918 these were divided between Austria and Czechoslovakia, and some were used by Rumania. In 1939 the type had been withdrawn from first-line use by Austria and Czechoslovakia but the type was taken over by the Germans as the 15 cm sFH 15(t) or (ö). They were used by front-line German artillery formations during the early war years but were then gradually withdrawn from use. The carriage of this piece was one of those used for trials with the 12.8 cm K 81.

Skoda 159 mm Model 25

DATA
CALIBRE 149.1 mm 5.87 in
LENGTH OF PIECE (L/18) 2700 mm
    106.3 in
WEIGHT IN ACTION 3740 kg 8247 lb
ELEVATION —5° to 72°
TRAVERSE 7°
M.V. 450 m/s 1476 lb
MAXIMUM RANGE 11,800 m 12,909 yards
SHELL WEIGHT 42 kg 92.6 lb

The Skoda M.25 was the first new design to be undertaken by them for the new Czech state and design work began during the early 1920s. The new howitzer was approved for service in 1925 and production continued until 1933. It was intended that the new piece would replace the existing M.14/16 but that existing stocks of ammunition would fit the new barrel. The resultant design was thus a compromise and as a result it lacked range and by the late 1930s it was scheduled for replacement by the Skoda M.37. The carriage was intended for horse traction only. To the Czech army the M.25 was known as the 15 cm hrubá houfnice vz.25. After the German take-over of 1938 and 1939 this piece entered Wehrmacht service as the 15 cm sFH 25(t) and was used widely by them, especially during the early campaigns of 1940 and 1941.

1
1. *15 cm hrubá houfnice vz. 25* **2.** *15 cm sFH 25 (t)*

2

Skoda 149 mm Model 33 (K1)

In the early 1930s Skoda introduced a new series of howitzers known as the 'K' series. The first of the series, the K1, was also known as the M.33. The M.33 was a good thoroughly modern design which incorporated a split trail and it was designed for horse or lorry traction. It could be towed either as a single load or in two separate loads with the barrel on a separate carriage. The M.33 was tested by the Czech army but not taken into service by them and the M.33 was offered for export. It was bought by Turkey, Rumania and Jugoslavia. To the Jugoslavs it was known as the M.36 but was bought in small numbers only. The Germans captured some of these in 1941 and kept them for use by occupation units as the 15 cm sFH 402(j).

DATA
CALIBRE   149.1 mm   5.87 in
LENGTH OF PIECE (L/27)   4050 mm   159.5. in
WEIGHT TRAVELLING (one load)   5820 kg   12,833 lb
WEIGHT IN ACTION   5020 kg   11,069 lb
ELEVATION   —5° to 70°
TRAVERSE   45°
M.V.   570 m/s   1870 ft/sec
MAXIMUM RANGE   15,100 m   16,250 yards
SHELL WEIGHT   42 kg   92.6 lb

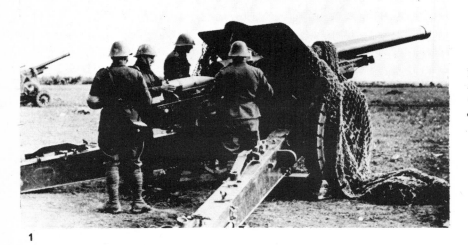

1. *A Skoda Model 33 in action with a Rumanian unit in Russia, 1941* 2. *Skoda 149 mm Model 33*

Skoda 149 mm Model 37 (K4)

Although the Czech army had not taken the Skoda K1 howitzer into service they were sufficiently impressed to fund further development of the series until the K4, which was designed for tractor towing only, was approved for service in 1937 after tests that began in 1936. It was intended that this piece, the M.37, would replace the M.25 in service but it was not until December 1938 that the first equipments were issued to the Czech army. Its intended designation was 15 cm hrubá houfnice vz.37 but the type was destined never to be used by the Czech army for soon after delivery Czechoslovakia was taken into the German sphere of influence and the M.37 was kept in production for the Wehrmacht as the 15 cm sFH 37(t). Some were issued to the Slovakian Army. The M.37 resembled the earlier M.33 in appearance but there were numerous changes to the carriage and the barrel was shorter.

DATA
CALIBRE   149.1 mm   5.87 in
LENGTH OF PIECE (L/24)   3600 mm   142 in
WEIGHT IN ACTION   5200 kg   11,466 lb
WEIGHT TRAVELLING   5730 kg   12,635 lb
ELEVATION   —5° to 70°
TRAVERSE   45°
M.V.   580 m/s   1903 ft/sec
MAXIMUM RANGE   15,100 m   16,520 yards
SHELL WEIGHT   42 kg   92.6 lb

1. *A 15 cm sFH 37(t) unit emplaced near Thermopoylae, 1941* 2. *15 cm hrubá houfnice vz. 37*

Skoda 149 mm Model 1928 (NOa)

DATA
CALIBRE 149.1 mm 5.87 in
LENGTH OF PIECE (L/46.5) 7025 mm
  276.6 in
WEIGHT IN ACTION (approx) 15,000 kg
  33,075 lb
ELEVATION 4° to 45°
TRAVERSE 360°
M.V. 760 m/s 2494 ft/sec
MAXIMUM RANGE 23,800 m 26,037 yards
SHELL WEIGHT 56 kg 123.5 lb

The Skoda M.28 was an export model of a heavy long range gun intended for firing against static fortifications that could also double as a coastal defence weapon. Although tested by the Czech army as the 15 cm kanon NOa it was not taken by them and was sold to Jugoslavia and Rumania. The M.28 was transported in three loads. When emplaced it had a full 360° traverse and was supported on a heavy metal platform. What number was sold to Rumania is not known, but about 20 were sold to Jugoslavia. There the gun was known as the 150 mm M.28 and formed the main striking power of the Jugoslav heavy artillery. After 1941 this gun was taken over by the Germans as the 15 cm K 403(j) and used by them in Russia and also as a coastal defence gun.

1

3

4

1. Skoda 149 mm Model 1928(NOa) as sold to Jugoslavia as the M.28 2. Model 1928 barrel on transporter 3. Model 1928 cradle on transporter 4. Model 1928 platform on transporter

Skoda 152 mm Model 15/16

DATA (Cannone da 152/37)
CALIBRE 152.4 mm 6 in
LENGTH OF PIECE (L/39.36) 6000 mm
  236.25 in
LENGTH OF BARREL 5581 mm 219.75 in
LENGTH OF RIFLING (L/29.15) 4442 mm
  174.9 in
WEIGHT IN ACTION 11,900 kg 26,240 lb
ELEVATION —6° to 45°
TRAVERSE 6°
M.V. (max) 700 m/s 2297 ft/sec
MAXIMUM RANGE 21,840 m 23,893 yards
SHELL WEIGHT 54 kg 119 lb

The design of a new 15 cm gun to replace a design dating from 1880 was initiated by the Austro-Hungarian Army before 1914. The initial results of their efforts was the Skoda M.15 which entered service in 1915 but only about 27 were produced before the elevation mechanism was revised to increase the possible elevation from 32° to 45°. This change resulted in the M.15/16 gun which then became one of the standard guns of the post-war Czech and Austrian armies. The Austrian guns had been withdrawn from use by the mid-1930s but the Czech guns were still in reserve use when the Germans took over in 1939. The few remaining pieces then became the 15 cm K 15/16(t). In 1939 another state that was still using the M.15/16 was Italy. The Italians had captured a number during World War 1 and by June 1940 there were still 29 in service as the Cannone da 152/37. These guns were used in Greece, Albania and Egypt but by September only 21 were left of which four were in Africa and the rest in Italy. These guns had been refurbished and fitted with new wheels by the firm of Vickers-Terni during the 1920s, and at the same time new liners and chambers had been fitted. In 1943 the guns on the Italian mainland became German property as the 15.2 cm K 410(i).

1. Emplacing a Cannone da 152/37 2,3. Skoda 152 mm Model 15/16 in service with the Czech Army 4. Cannone da 152/37(P.B.) seen here fitted with a shield 5. 15 cm K 15/16(t) emplaced as a coastal gun 6. Cannone da 152/37

1

2

3

4

5

6

Skoda 21 cm Model 18 and 18/19

DATA (21 cm M.18)
CALIBRE 210 mm 8.27 in
LENGTH OF PIECE (L/16) 3360 mm 132 in
WEIGHT OF PIECE 9460 kg 20860 lb
ELEVATION 40° to 71° 30′
TRAVERSE 360°
M.V. 380 m/s 1247 ft/sec
MAXIMUM RANGE 10,100 m 11,050 yards
SHELL WEIGHT 135 kg 297.7 lb

Before and during World War 1 the heavy howitzers produced by Skoda for the Austro-Hungarian Army were of 149 and 305 mm. It was felt that an interim 210 mm calibre weapon would be useful and the result was the 21 cm M.16, a horse-drawn howitzer referred to as a Morser (Mrs). The M.16 could be broken down into as many as five loads but the Austro-Hungarian Army technical committee felt that there was little need for such a weapon to be fired from a mobile carriage and that such a heavy weapon should have a longer range than the M.16. The result was that the L/14 barrel of the M.16 was lengthened to L/16 and a new projectile and increased charge cartridge were developed to produce the M.18 which fired from a platform. After 1918 this howitzer served with the Czech Army as the 21 cm mozdir vz.18. Despite the intention that the M.18 was to be a static weapon, a further development was the 21 cm M.18/19 which was a mobile version intended from the start to be towed by a lorry. By 1939 the M.16 had passed from the scene but the M.18 and M.18/19 passed into German service as the 21 cm Mrs M 18(t) and 21 cm Mrs 18/19(t).

1. Skoda 21 cm Model 18 2. Skoda 21 cm Model 18/19 3. 21 cm Mrs 18/19(t) mounted on its transporter

1

2

3

Skoda 210 mm Model 1939

1939 was the high-water mark in Soviet-German relations before the Invasion of 1941 set the two nations at war. In August 1939 the two nations signed a political and trade agreement in which the Russians agreed to trade raw materials and wheat in exchange for various manufactured goods, among which were armaments. The political part of the agreement lead to the invasion of Poland by both nations and the trade section resulted in a number of arms deals among which the Germans provided Russia with heavy artillery. The heavy artillery supplied was built by Skoda under German supervision and consisted of a 210 mm gun and a 305 mm howitzer both of which used the same carriage, firing platform and control mechanism. The 210 mm gun was the Skoda Model 1939 which became known to the Russians as the BR-17. It was a large heavy piece suited to static long-range anti-emplacement work and on the road it was carried in three loads. Rate of fire was one round every three minutes. The exact number supplied to the Russians is unknown but cannot have been very high as there are no records of any being captured by the Germans after 1941. Their records make reference to a 21 cm K 521(r) but it cannot be confirmed that any were used by them as this designation was issued for reporting reasons only.

Skoda 21 cm K52

The Skoda 21 cm K52 gun had its origins in a design produced to a Turkish order in 1938. Apparently two guns were made and delivered before the Czech armament industry was taken over by the Germans, and the type was kept in production for the Wehrmacht as the 21 cm Kanone 39. The K39 saw service in Russia and some other theatres during 1941 and 1942 and by then the need for heavy artillery in the German artillery park was so pressing that a further version was ordered under the Skoda design designation of K52. This version was essentially similar to the earlier gun but was generally simplified and a muzzle brake was added, making this gun the largest in German service to be fitted with this feature. The revised design became the 21 cm K39/40 and twenty were built and delivered. In 1944 a further forty were ordered, again with revisions to the basic design but only sixteen had been made by April 1945. This last batch became the 21 cm K 39/41. The basic K52 design was sound but unremarkable and differed from other guns built for the Germans in having an interrupted screw breech block instead of the usual sliding block. Despite the various design changes the performance was unchanged from the first model. The rate of fire was slow even for a gun of this size as the barrel had to be loaded at an elevation of 8° which usually meant relaying between shots. Time into action was between six to eight hours.

DATA
CALIBRE 210 mm 8.27 in
LENGTH OF PIECE (approx) 10,058 mm 396 in
WEIGHT IN ACTION 43,218 kg 95,195 lb
ELEVATION —6° to 50°
TRAVERSE 22°
M.V. 800 m/s 2624 ft/sec
MAXIMUM RANGE 30,450 m 33,278 yards
SHELL WEIGHT 134.8 kg 297 lb

Skoda 210 mm Model 1939 as supplied to the Russians

DATA
CALIBRE 210 mm 8.27 in
LENGTH OF PIECE (L/45) 9530 mm 375.2 in
WEIGHT IN ACTION 33,800 kg 74,530 lb
ELEVATION —4° to 45°
TRAVERSE 360°
M.V. (no muzzle brake) 800 m/s 2625 ft/sec
M.V. (with muzzle brake) 860 m/s 2822 ft/sec
MAXIMUM RANGE 30,000 m 32,820 yards
SHELL WEIGHT (HE) 135 kg 297.7 lb

21 cm K 39/41

FRANCE

Schneider 107 mm Canon mle 10/12

DATA
CALIBRE   106.7 mm   4.2 in
LENGTH OF PIECE (L/28)   2995 mm   118 in
WEIGHT TRAVELLING   2486 kg   5482 lb
WEIGHT IN ACTION   2172 kg   4790 lb
ELEVATION   —5° to 37°
TRAVERSE   6°
M.V.   570 m/s   1870 ft/sec
MAXIMUM RANGE   12,500 m   13,675 yards
SHELL WEIGHT   16.3 kg   36.16 lb

In 1910 Schneider produced a 107 mm field gun to a Russian order and as far as can be discovered it was built under licence at the Putilov arsenal. In service it was discovered that modifications were necessary to the carriage and after these had been embodied the gun became known as the 10/12 S. By the late 1920s it was decided to update the gun by using a longer barrel on the same carriage and these guns then became the 107-10/30 (refer to Russian section), but in 1941 some equipments had still not been updated and were still in use by training and other second-line units. For reporting purposes the Germans gave this gun the designation 10.7 cm K 351(r) but they do not appear to have used them for any purpose as they preferred the later model. In use the 10/12 S was towed by eight horses.

107-10/30

Canon de 145 L mle 1916 St Chamond

DATA
CALIBRE   145 mm   5.7 in
LENGTH OF PIECE (L/50.8)   7362 mm
   289.8 in
LENGTH OF BARREL   7362 mm   289.8 in
LENGTH OF RIFLING   6112.8 mm   240.66 in
WEIGHT TRAVELLING   14,060 kg   31,002 lb
WEIGHT IN ACTION   13,210 kg   29,128 lb
ELEVATION   0° to 38°
TRAVERSE   6°
M.V.   784 m/s   2572 ft/sec
MAXIMUM RANGE   20,200 m   22,100 yards
SHELL WEIGHT   36.2 kg   79.82 lb

During 1916 the Battle of Verdun soon turned into an artillery battle of unforeseen magnitude and revealed to the French Army their lack of heavy guns suitable to counter the German heavy weapons. In an attempt to use existing barrels the French Arsenal of St. Chamond took a number of 145 mm naval gun barrels and placed them on a land carriage to produce what was called the L 16 St Ch. After 1918 there were many of these guns left, usually emplaced in time as coastal defence guns, and in 1939 there were still 215 left in service. When any barrels became worn with use they were rebored to 155 mm to become the Canon de 155 L mle 1916 St Chamond. In its 145 mm version after 1940 the L 16 St Ch became the German 14.5 cm K 405 (f). Rumania obtained a batch of these 145 mm guns but when and in what quantities is unknown.

1-4. *Canon de 145 L mle 1916 St Chamond*

1

2

3

4

Schneider 149 mm Obusier mle 1929

Normally the German Krupp concern supplied the bulk of the Danish artillery requirements but during the late 1920s the terms of the Versailles Treaty were still in force and thus the Germans were not in a position to meet an order to update the Danish artillery park. The order went instead to the French Schneider concern who produced a heavy field howitzer, the mle 1929, to fire existing stocks of ammunition. In service this piece was known as the M.29 L/22 S and it used the same carriage as the 10.5 cm mle 1930 field gun. This carriage was a rather heavy split trail affair intended for towing by either horse or tractor. At the same time a small number of 155 mm howitzers were delivered using a box trail, and these guns were used by the Danes under the same designation as the 149 mm guns. It would also appear that some of the 149 mm barrels were later rebored to the 155 mm calibre, but in 1940 both types came under the German fold. The 149 mm guns then became the 15 cm sFH 461(d) and were used to equip occupation units. Very few of the 155 mm guns appear to have fallen into German hands as there is no record of any being used by them but a reporting designation of 15.5 cm sFH 469(d) was issued.

DATA (149 mm version)
CALIBRE   149.1 mm   5.87 in
LENGTH OF PIECE (L/22)   3280 mm   129 in
WEIGHT TRAVELLING   5675 kg   12,513 lb
WEIGHT IN ACTION   5165 kg   11,389 lb
ELEVATION   0° to 45°
TRAVERSE   40°
M.V.   635 m/s   2083 ft/sec
MAXIMUM RANGE   15,000 m   16,400 yards
SHELL WEIGHT   38.4 kg   84.67 lb

1

2

1. *Schneider 149 mm Obusier mle 1929* 2. *Schneider 155 mm Obusier mle 1929*

Schneider Canon de 152 mle 1910

DATA
CALIBRE   152.4 mm   6 in
LENGTH OF PIECE (L/28)   4260 mm   167.7 in
WEIGHT IN ACTION   4000 kg   8820 lb
ELEVATION   —5° to 40°
TRAVERSE   4° 30′
M.V.   640 m/s   2100 ft/sec
MAXIMUM RANGE   12,400 m   13,565 yards
SHELL WEIGHT   40.9 kg   90.18 lb

The gun produced in 152 mm calibre to a Russian order in 1910 was licence-built by the Putilov Arsenal for the Russian Army after only a few prototypes had been produced in France. After 1910 this gun may be regarded as a Russian weapon as it formed the basis for a line of Russian guns. The 10S, as it was known to the Russians, was designed for two-part travelling over long distances and the carriage and limber could be fitted with wheels suitable for horse or tractor towing. After service in World War 1 the gun continued in service and a new range of ammunition was developed to increase the range. After 1930 many barrels were reconditioned and placed on a new carriage to produce the 152-10/30 but in 1941 when the Germans invaded there were still unconverted guns in use with second-line units. These were taken into the German fold as the 15.2 cm K 435(r) but they were little used by the Germans, if at all, and it would seem safe to assume that they were scrapped. The data should be considered as provisional.

Canon de 155 L mle 1916 St Chamond

DATA
CALIBRE   155 mm   6.1 in
LENGTH OF PIECE (L/47.5)   7362 mm
   289.8 in
LENGTH OF BARREL   7262 mm   289.8 in
LENGTH OF RIFLING   5871.5 mm   231.16 in
WEIGHT TRAVELLING   14,000 kg   30,870 lb
WEIGHT IN ACTION   13,150 kg   28,996 lb
ELEVATION   0° to 38°
TRAVERSE   6°
M.V.   790 m/s   2592 ft/sec
MAXIMUM RANGE   21,300 m   23,300 yards
SHELL WEIGHT   43 kg   94.8 lb

This gun was a rebored version of the 145 mm mle 1916 St Chamond naval gun produced during World War 1. As the 145 mm barrels became worn they were rebored to the standard French Army calibre of 155 mm. They continued to use the same carriage as the earlier gun and in 1939 many were still in use as fortification and coastal defence guns. At some time between the wars a batch was sent to Italy where they were used under the designation of Cannone da 155/45 PB. They fired a heavier shell than the French guns—47 kg (103.6 lb) as opposed to 43 kg (94.8 lb). After 1940 the French guns became the German 15.5 cm K 420(f) and after 1943 the few remaining Italian guns became the 15.5 cm K 420(i).

A captured 15.5 cm K 420(f) at Gatteville, July 1944

Canon de 155 L mle 1877-1914 Schneider

The L 77/14 S was a hurried conversion of the elderly mle 1877 barrel to enable it to be mounted on the carriage of the Schneider mle 1910 152 mm gun produced for export to Russia. A recoil system was fitted to the barrel and the result was an adequate field gun that helped to provide some form of heavy gun when it was needed most. By 1939 the mle 1877-1914 had been relegated to the role of fortress gun and armed many of the various garrison towns of France. In 1940 many of them were taken into German service and were used both as coastal defence guns and also as field guns for units based in France. The German designation was 15.5 cm K 422(f). At some date prior to 1939 the Russians had also received a batch of these guns.

DATA
CALIBRE   155 mm   6.1 in
LENGTH OF PIECE (L/27)   4200 mm
   165.35 in
LENGTH OF BARREL   4110 mm   161.8 in
LENGTH OF RIFLING   3171 mm   124.84 in
WEIGHT IN ACTION   6010 kg   13,252 lb
ELEVATION   —5° to 42°
TRAVERSE   4° 40′
M.V.   561 m/s   1840 ft/sec
MAXIMUM RANGE   13,900 m   15,200 yards
SHELL WEIGHT   42.9 kg   94.6 lb

Canon de 155 C mle 15 St Chamond

Designed in 1914 to a specification requiring a more modern design of howitzer to fire existing stocks of ammunition, the mle 1915 entered service in 1915. Its general title was C 15 St Ch and a total of 390 were built before the Schneider C 17 S was ready for service. In 1939 many of these howitzers were still in use and after 1940 the Germans took them over as the 15.5 cm sFH 415(f). The C 15 St Ch was an unremarkable design but it was an adequate performer and took the field with the Germans in 1941. It remained in use in 1944 when the Allied forces landed in France.

DATA
CALIBRE   155 mm   6.1 in
LENGTH OF PIECE (L/17.8)   2764 mm
   108.8 in
LENGTH OF BARREL   2517 mm   99 in
LENGTH OF RIFLING   2255 mm   88.78 in
WEIGHT TRAVELLING   3860 kg   8511 lb
WEIGHT IN ACTION   3040 kg   6703 lb
ELEVATION   —5° to 40°
TRAVERSE   5° 40′
M.V.   467 m/s   1204 ft/sec
MAXIMUM RANGE   10,600 m   11,596 yards
SHELL WEIGHT   43.5 kg   95.9 lb

Canon de 155 C mle 1917 Schneider

The conditions of the Western Front during World War 1 virtually dictated the design of the Schneider 155 mm mle 1917, or C 17 S as it was usually known. It entered service during 1917 and soon proved itself to be a most useful and sturdy weapon that became one of the best designs from any nation to be used in that conflict. It was soon taken into the American Army inventory and after World War 1 was over it was exported to a host of nations. As a result it was still in service with many states in 1939, not the least of which was France herself, for in that year there were still 2043 in service. The Russian guns had been sleeved to take the standard Russian 152 mm calibre. Any guns that were captured by the Germans were used by them for a variety of purposes which ranged from standard field artillery issue to coastal defence, and the listing below of the main users gives the eventual German designation.

Belgium: Obusier de 155   *15.5 cm sFH 413(b)*
Brazil:
France: Canon de 155 C mle 1917 Schneider   *15.5 cm sFH 414(f)*
Finland:
Greece: M.17
Italy: Obice da 155/14 PB   *15.5 cm sFH 414(i)*
Jugoslavia: M.17
Poland: 155 mm haubica wz. 1917   *15.5 cm sFH 17(p)*
Rumania:
USA: 155 mm Howitzer M1917 & 1917A1
USSR: 152-17S   *15.2 cm sFH 449(r)*

DATA (C 17 S)
CALIBRE 155 mm 6.1 in
LENGTH OF PIECE (L/15.3) 2332 mm
91.8 in
LENGTH OF BARREL 2176 mm 85.67 in
LENGTH OF RIFLING 1737 mm 68.385 in
WEIGHT TRAVELLING 3720 kg 8203 lb
WEIGHT IN ACTION 3300 kg 7277 lb
ELEVATION 0° to 42° 20′
TRAVERSE 6°
M.V. 450 m/s 1476 ft/sec
MAXIMUM RANGE 11,300 m 12,362 yards
SHELL WEIGHT 43.61 kg 96.16 lb

1,2,4. Canon de 155 mle 1917 Schneider
3. Obice da 155/14 PB

1

2   3

4

A Greek M.17 in action near the Albanian border, October 1940

Canon de 155 L mle 1917 Schneider

In 1917 the need for longer range heavy guns was so pressing that the French had to resort to placing a new L/31.9 barrel in the place of the elderly L/27 barrel of the ageing Canon de 155 L mle 1877-1914. A total of 410 conversions were made and the type served on until 1940. Between the wars a batch was sent to Belgium, and this batch retained its general French designation of Can 155 L 17 S. By 1939 many of these guns had been converted for motor traction vy the addition of rubber tyres. In 1940 these guns passed into German service as the 15.5. cm K 416(f) and 416(b), although some of the Belgian guns were referred to as the 15.5 cm K 431(b).

DATA
CALIBRE   155 mm   6.1 in
LENGTH OF PIECE (L/31.91)   4950 mm   194.88 in
LENGTH OF BARREL   4680 mm   184.25 in
LENGTH OF RIFLING   3691 mm   145.3 in
WEIGHT TRAVELLING (one load)   9900 kg   21,830 lb
WEIGHT TRAVELLING (two loads)   12,170 kg   26,835 lb
WEIGHT IN ACTION   8956 kg   19,748 lb
ELEVATION   —5° to 40°
TRAVERSE   4° 30′
M.V.   665 m/s   2182 ft/sec
MAXIMUM RANGE   17,300 m   18,925 yards
SHELL WEIGHT   43 kg   94.8 lb

A 15.5 cm K 416(f) emplaced as a coastal defence gun

Canon de 155 L mle 1918 Schneider

DATA
CALIBRE 155 mm 6.1 in
LENGTH OF PIECE (L/26.4) 4089 mm
 161 in
LENGTH OF RIFLING 3171 mm 124.84 in
WEIGHT TRAVELLING 5530 kg 12,194 lb
WEIGHT IN ACTION 5050 kg 11,135 lb
ELEVATION 1° 15′ to 43° 35′
TRAVERSE 6°
M.V. 561 m/s 1840 ft/sec
MAXIMUM RANGE 13,600 m 14,880 yards
SHELL WEIGHT 43.1 kg 95 lb

Another of the many extemporised field peices turned out by the French during World War 1 was the Can 155 L 18 S. This was yet another variation produced by placing the old Mle 1877/1914 barrel on an improvised carriage, this time that of the C 17 S. No shield was fitted and the barrel was slightly revised from the original. In 1939 it was still in service and was captured by the Germans in sufficient numbers to enter their service as the 15.5 cm K 425 (f).

Canon de 155 Grand Puissance Filloux

DATA
CALIBRE 155 mm 6.1 in
LENGTH OF PIECE (L/38.2) 5915 mm
 232.87 in
LENGTH OF BARREL 5725 mm 225.4 in
LENGTH OF RIFLING 4583 mm 180.4 in
WEIGHT TRAVELLING 11,700 kg 25,800 lb
WEIGHT IN ACTION 10,750 kg 23,704 lb
ELEVATION 0° to 35°
TRAVERSE 60°
M.V. 735 m/sec 2411 ft/sec
MAXIMUM RANGE 19,500 m 21,330 yards
SHELL WEIGHT 43 kg 94.8 lb

The Canon de 155 GPF was first used in action in 1917 and was a most useful and successful weapon. It was one of the guns selected for use by the American contingent in France in 1918 and after then remained in service with the US Army until World War 2 as the 155 mm Gun M1918M1 (please refer). In French service this gun was usually known as the Can 155 GPF, and in 1939 there were still 449 in service. In 1940 large numbers of these were taken over by the Germans as the 15.5 cm K 418(f). They valued them highly and used them both as 'standard' field guns and eventually as coastal defence weapons. Not all the French guns were captured however, for some were used in the 1943 Italian campaigns by Polish troops.

Above and below: *15.5 cm K 418(f)*

Canon de 155 Grand Puissance Filloux—CA

This version of the basic Can 155 GPF gun was identical in appearance but it had a different chamber length and fired a different type of ammunition. It was known as the Can 155 GPF-CA. By 1939 few were left in service and after 1940 this version was not taken into service by the Germans as its performance was not as good as the normal Can 155 GPF. However, any that were statically emplaced remained in German use as the 15.5 cm K 417(f) until their ammunition was expended.

DATA
CALIBRE   155 mm   6.1 in
LENGTH OF PIECE (L/38.2)   5915 mm
  232.87 in
LENGTH OF BARREL   5725 mm   225.4 in
LENGTH OF RIFLING (approx)   4283 mm
  168.6 in
WEIGHT IN ACTION   10,750 kg   23,704 lb
ELEVATION   0° to 35°
TRAVERSE   60°
M.V.   721 m/s   2365 ft/sec
MAXIMUM RANGE   16,500 m   18,050 yards
SHELL WEIGHT   44.85 kg   98.9 lb

DATA
As Canon de 155 GPF except for:—
WEIGHT TRAVELLING   13,800 kg   30,430 lb
WEIGHT IN ACTION   unknown

Canon de 155 Grand Puissance Filloux—Touzzard

The Can 155 GPF-T was a modernised version of the basic Can 155 GPF, but differed mainly in having a new carriage which travelled on six pneumatic wheels. In action it rested on four of these wheels. This new carriage was suitable for motor traction and in 1939 it was gradually being retrofitted to existing Can 155 GPF equipments. After 1940 this weapon entered the German inventory as the 15.5 cm K 419(f) as a prized acquisition. The carriage was later used for the 12.8 cm K 81/1.

Canon de 155 L mle 1932 Schneider

Produced to fulfil a French Army requirement which called for a more modern gun than the numerous rather short range guns that made up the bulk of the French artillery arm. The result was the Can 155 L 32 S which had a most useful range and had a good modern and mobile carriage. When emplaced the Can 155 L mle 32 S had a full 360° traverse. After the 1940 campaign this gun passed into German service as the 15.5 cm K 424(f).

DATA
CALIBRE   155 mm   6.1 in
LENGTH OF PIECE (L/55)   27,500 mm
  1082.8 in
WEIGHT IN ACTION   16,400 kg   36,162 lb
ELEVATION   —8° to 45°
TRAVERSE EMPLACED   360°
M.V.   900 m/s   2953 ft/sec
MAXIMUM RANGE   27,500 m   30,085 yards
SHELL WEIGHT   50 kg   110.25 lb

GERMANY

Krupp 10.7 cm K 08/10

In 1908 Russia bought a batch of 10.7 cm guns from Krupps which entered Russian service as the 08/10 Kp. The numbers involved are uncertain but do not appear to have been large as this model lacked range for a gun of its calibre and soon after the Russians ordered a similar French Schneider gun upon which they standardised. In 1941 there were still some of these elderly weapons in use with various second-line units but any the Germans captured were not pressed into German service as they probably regarded them as obsolete for modern warfare. The data below should be regarded as provisional.

DATA
CALIBRE 106.7 mm 4.2 in
LENGTH OF PIECE (L/30) 3210 mm 126 in
WEIGHT TRAVELLING 2500 kg 5510 lb
WEIGHT IN ACTION 2200 kg 4850 lb
ELEVATION —5° to 30°
TRAVERSE 6°
M.V. 560 m/s 1837 ft/sec
MAXIMUM RANGE 9500 m 10,390 yards
SHELL WEIGHT 16.4 kg 36.16 lb

Rheinmetall 12 cm leFH 08

This gun was produced by Rheinmetall to a Norwegian order in 1908 and it entered service in the following year as the M.09. In 1939 it was still in use and although it had been supplemented by later models still made up part of the total of 24 field howitzers used by the three batteries of the single heavy artillery battalion of the Norwegian Army. These guns were given the reporting designation of 12 cm leFH 375(n) by the Germans but there are no records of them being used in German service and it seems very likely that they were scrapped. The data below should be regarded as provisional.

DATA
CALIBRE 120 mm 4.72 in
LENGTH OF PIECE (L/20) 2400 mm 94.5 in
WEIGHT IN ACTION 1360 kg 3000 lb
ELEVATION —5° to 45°
TRAVERSE 54°
M.V. 300 m/s 985 ft/sec
MAXIMUM RANGE 6100 m 6675 yards
SHELL WEIGHT 20.4 kg 45 lb

1

1. Norwegian 12 cm M.09 **2.** *Rheinmetall 12 cm leFHO8*

2

12.8 cm Kanone 44

The Russian Front upset many German precepts as the early advances of 1941 faded into memory. One precept that was soon shattered was that German artillery equipment was superior to the Russian equivalents, for the extremely efficient Russian medium guns soon revealed shortcomings in the standard German artillery. In an attempt to counter this state of affairs Krupps designed the 12.8 cm K 43 which was a light gun with a screw breech instead of the normal German sliding block. This design was soon passed over in favour of the 12.8 cm K 44 for which both Krupps and Rheinmetall designed prototypes. This advanced design was a dual purpose weapon (anti-tank and field piece) mounted on a 360° carriage, and was often referred to as the 12.8 cm Pak 44. Both guns emerged as very similar in performance but the four-wheeled Krupp carriage was preferred to the more complex six-wheeled carriage of the Rheinmetall entry. A version of the Krupp carriage was intended for use with the projected 15 cm sFH 44, and a tank version of the K 44 was the 12.8 cm KwK 82 mounted in the Jagdtiger. Despite the excellent performance of the K 44 prolonged production difficulties prevented many reaching the front line and very few were produced.

DATA (Krupp version)
CALIBRE 128 mm 5.04 in
LENGTH OF PIECE (L/54.8) 7023 mm 276.5 in
LENGTH OF BARREL 6625mm 260.8 in
LENGTH OF RIFLING 5550 mm 218.5 in
WEIGHT IN ACTION 10,160 kg 22,403 lb
ELEVATION —7° 51′ to 45° 27′
TRAVERSE 360°
M.V. 920 m/s 3018 ft/sec
MAXIMUM RANGE 24,414 m 26,709 yards
SHELL WEIGHT (HE & AP) 28.3 kg 62.4 lb

1,2. 12.8 cm K 44—Krupp version **3,4.** *12.8cm K 44—Rheinmetall version*

1

2

3

4

12.8 cm Kanone 81

While the K 44 was intended as a field gun with an anti-tank capability, a development known as the 12.8 cm K 81 was intended as a true dual-purpose weapon. It was intended that a mobile cruciform carriage similar to that of the K 44 but production of this mounting was so slow that none reached the field. The only K 81 guns that actually saw action were mounted on captured carriages. The most numerous of these conversions was the 12.8 cm K 81/1 which used the carriage of the French Canon de 155 GPF-T (15.5 cm K 419(f)). This combination was not a great success as the carriage was really too light for the task and it proved difficult to tow. Another version of the K 81 was the 12.8 cm K 81/2 which used the carriage of the Russian 152-1937 (15.2 cm KH 433/1(r)) but this conversion was even less successful than the K 81/1. Despite their shortcomings both conversions were used in action as the last winter of the war dragged through its final stages. Trial conversions that did not see service used the following carriages:—

Skoda M.15 (15 cm sFH 15(t))
Skoda M.14/16 (15 cm sFH 14/16(t))
Obice da 149/12 modello 14 (15 cm sFH 400(i))
15 cm sFH 13
15 cm sFH 16

DATA (K 81/1)
CALIBRE   128 mm   5.04 in
LENGTH OF PIECE (L/54.85)   7020 mm   276.37 in
LENGTH OF RIFLING   5533 mm   217.83 in
WEIGHT IN ACTION   12,197 kg   26,894 lb
ELEVATION   —4° to 45°
TRAVERSE   60°
M.V.   920 m/s   3018 ft/sec
MAXIMUM RANGE   24,414 m   26,709 yards
SHELL WEIGHT   28.3 kg   62.4 lb

1

2

1,2. *12.8 cm K 81/1*

15 cm schwere Feldhaubitze 13

DATA

CALIBRE 149.7 mm 5.89 in
LENGTH OF PIECE (L/17) 2550 mm 100.4 in
LENGTH OF RIFLING 2054 mm 80.866 in
WEIGHT IN ACTION 2250 kg 4961 lb
WEIGHT TRAVELLING (approx) 3000 kg 6615 lb
ELEVATION —5° to 45°
TRAVERSE 9°
M.V. 381 m/s 1250 ft/sec
MAXIMUM RANGE 8600 m 9408 yards
SHELL WEIGHT 40.8 kg 89.96 lb
Self-propelled carriages
15 cm sFH 13 Selbsfahrlafette Lorraine (SdKfz 135/1)

In 1917 when the sFH 14 was first issued to the heavy batteries of the German Army it was one of the finest guns of its class in service. In 1919 it featured in war reparations to Belgium and Holland—in Belgium it became the Obusier de 150 L/17 while in Holland it continued to be known as the 15 cm sFH. By 1939 very few of these war reparation guns remained in service with Belgium and Holland but the type was still used by the Wehrmacht. The sFH 13 was a Krupp design intended for horse traction which meant after 1939 that the type was used in a static or coastal role only, but in 1942 a total of 102 guns were mounted on an obsolete captured French tracked carrier chassis to provide a measure of mobile heavy artillery for units based in France. Captured Belgian guns became the 15 cm sFH 409(b) and Dutch guns became the 15 cm sFH 406(h).

Obusier de 150 L/17

15 cm Kanone 16

DATA (15 cm K 16 Kp)

CALIBRE 149.3 mm 5.878 in
LENGTH OF PIECE (L/42.7) 6400 mm 252 in
LENGTH OF BARREL (L/40.1) 6020 mm 237 in
WEIGHT IN ACTION 10,180 kg 22,445 lb
ELEVATION 0° to 46°
TRAVERSE 8°
M.V. 744 m/s 2440 ft/sec
MAXIMUM RANGE 22,000 m 24,070 yards
SHELL WEIGHT 50.223 kg 110.74 lb

The 15 cm K 16 was produced during World War 1 in two almost identical versions. These two versions were built by Rheinmetall and Krupp and each was known as either the K 16 Rh or K 16 Kp and differed only in various dimensions and weights —for instance the Krupp barrel was L/42.7 long while the Rheinmetall barrel measured L/42.9. In 1939 the German Army still used some of these guns but as they had been designed for horse traction they were used mainly in static roles or for training. The ammunition fired by this gun was different from the standard 15 cm ammunition which did not help the supply situation so gradually the K 16 was relegated to a coastal role. However, a small number of K 16 barrels were placed onto the carriage of the 21 cm Mrs 18 to become the 15 cm K 16 in Mrs Laf— this was only a stop-gap measure to provide some form of mobile heavy gun quickly during 1941. In 1919 a batch of 15 cm K 16 guns was handed over to Belgium in the shape of war reparations and in 1939 these were still in use. To the Belgians they were known as the Canon de 150 L/43. They formed part of the twenty-four strong heavy gun strength of the Belgian artillery park, but after 1940 they passed under German control as the 15 cm K 429(b). The Germans do not appear to have used them for any purpose and it seems very likely that they were scrapped.

15 cm K 16 seen here with rubber-tyred wheels

15 cm K 16

15 cm schwere Feldhaubitze 18

The 10 cm K 18 and the 15 cm sFH 18 were developed alongside each other during 1926-30. Rheinmetall developed both barrels but the common carriage was a Krupp responsibility. Both entered service during 1933 and 1934 and were intended to become the 'standard' pieces of the Wehrmacht medium and heavy artillery units. The sFH 18 was a good modern design with split trails carried on a small two-wheeled limber which enabled it to be towed by horses or by a tractor. A wide range of ammunition could be fired but range was lacking compared with such adversaries as the Russian 152 mm guns. Thus in 1942 an extra two charges were added to the six already in use to boost performance. These extra charges shortened the barrel life considerably and overstrained the recoil mechanism to the extent that a renewable chamber liner was developed and a muzzle brake fitted. Guns with these new features were known as the 15 cm sFH 18(M). A further variant was the 15 cm sFH 18/1 intended for mounting on mobile platforms, and this was further developed into the Panzerhaubitze 18/1 and Panzerfeldhaubitze 18M both of which were mounted on the Hummel. Some sFH 18 pieces were handed over to Finland after that state came under German influence and the type was used by them as the m/40. The Italian Army also used a number of sFH 18s which they knew as the Obice da 149/28.

Belgian Canon de 150 L/43 showing the original form of the carriage and wheels

DATA
CALIBRE   149 mm   5.87 in
LENGTH OF PIECE (L/29.6)   4440 mm
   174.8 in
LENGTH OF RIFLING   3623 mm   142.63 in
WEIGHT IN ACTION   5512 kg   12,154 lb
ELEVATION   —3° to 45°
TRAVERSE   64°
M.V. (maximum)   520 m/s   1710 ft/sec
MAXIMUM RANGE   13,325 m   14,600 yards
SHELL WEIGHT   43.5 kg   95.7 lb
Self-propelled carriages
Geschützwagen III/IV Hummel
   (SdKfz 165)

15 cm sFH 18(M)

A 15 cm sFH 18 fitted with light wheels for horse traction

Obice da 149/28

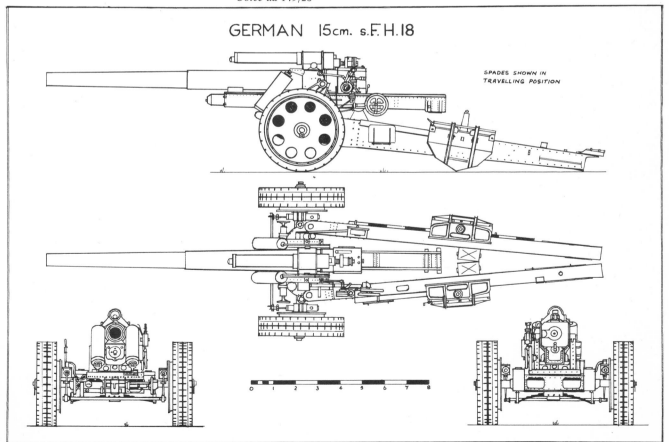

GERMAN 15cm. s.F.H.18

SPADES SHOWN IN
TRAVELLING POSITION

0 1 2 3 4 5 6 7 8

15 cm schwere Feldhaubitze 18/40 (42)

In 1938 the 15 cm sFH 40 was developed from the 15 cm sFH 36 which was itself an attempt to improve on the existing 15 cm sFH 18. Neither of the two new equipments was accepted for service as production priority had to be given to existing models. The development work was not entirely wasted for a total of 46 sFH 40 barrels were mounted on sFH 18 carriages and the result became the 15 cm sFH 18/40, later to be known as the sFH 42. The sFH 18/40 was fitted with a muzzle brake but this could not alter the fact that the hybrid was not as accurate as its predecessor and it was not a success in service.

DATA
CALIBRE   149 mm   5.87 in
LENGTH OF PIECE (L/32.5)   4875 mm   191.93 in
LENGTH OF RIFLING   3927 mm   154.61 in
WEIGHT IN ACTION   5720 kg   12,613 lb
ELEVATION   0° to 45°
TRAVERSE   56°
M.V. (maximum)   595 m/s   1952 ft/sec
MAXIMUM RANGE   15,100 m   16,514 yards
SHELL WEIGHT   43.5 kg   95.7 lb

15 cm sFH 36   *15 cm sFH 18/40*

15 cm Kanone 18

Development of what was intended to be the standard Wehrmacht heavy gun was started in 1933 by Rheinmetall-Borsig. The finished product entered service in 1938 as the 15 cm K 18 and had several unusual features. One feature was the use of a two-piece platform onto which the gun had to be hauled to give a 360° traverse. Another less useful feature was that the gun had to be towed in two sections which involved considerable time and labour getting the gun in and out of action. The K 18 remained in service until 1945 as the standard heavy gun of the Wehrmacht divisional artillery but as time went on it was gradually supplemented by heavier guns.

DATA
CALIBRE   149.1 mm   5.87 in
LENGTH OF PIECE (L/55)   8200 mm   322.8 in
LENGTH OF RIFLING   6432 mm   253.23 in
WEIGHT IN ACTION   12,760 kg   28,136 lb
ELEVATION   —2° to 45°
TRAVERSE ON PLATFORM   360°
TRAVERSE OFF PLATFORM   10°
M.V.   890 m/s   2920 ft/sec
MAXIMUM RANGE   24,500 m   26,800 yards
SHELL WEIGHT (HE)   43 kg   94.8 lb
SHELL WEIGHT (anti-concrete)   43.5 kg   95.9 lb

15 cm K 18 barrel on transporter

15 cm K 18 carriage

15 cm K 39

15 cm Kanone 39

The 15 cm K 39 came to the Wehrmacht by way of a frustrated Krupp development contract placed by Turkey. After September 1939 the guns that had been produced could not be delivered so in 1940 they were taken over by the Wehrmacht. The K 39 was a dual-purpose weapon that could be used as a heavy field gun or coastal defence gun. As a field gun the K 39 used a normal split trail but in the coastal defence role a portable turntable carried on a special transporter was employed. When mounted on this turntable the trails were joined and the piece could then be traversed through 360° by turning a geared handle. Using the turntable involved a considerable amount of digging-in. On the road the K 39 was carried in three loads, barrel and transporter, carriage, and platform and transporter. It remained in production until the war ended.

DATA
CALIBRE   149.1 mm   5.87 in
LENGTH OF PIECE (L/55)   8255 mm   325 in
LENGTH OF BARREL   7868 mm   309.7 in
LENGTH OF RIFLING   6505 mm   256.1 in
WEIGHT IN ACTION (field role)   12,200 kg   26,901 lb
ELEVATION   —3° to 46°
TRAVERSE ON TURNTABLE   360°
TRAVERSE OFF TURNTABLE   60°
M.V.   865 m/s   2838 ft/sec
MAXIMUM RANGE   24,700 m   27,022 yards
SHELL WEIGHT   43 kg   94.8 lb

15 cm K 39 on test

15 cm Schiffskanone C/28 in Morserlafette

In 1941 production of the 17 cm K 18 barrel was delayed at a time when they were badly needed in the field. As a typical stop-gap measure eight SK C/28 naval gun barrels were diverted from their intended purpose as coastal weapons and were mounted on the carriage of the 21 cm Mrs 18.

DATA
CALIBRE   149.1 mm   5.87 in
LENGTH OF PIECE (L/55)   8291 mm   326.4 in
LENGTH OF BARREL   7815 mm   307.7 in
LENGTH OF RIFLING   6584 mm   259.2 in
WEIGHT IN ACTION   16,870 kg   37,198 lb
ELEVATION   0° to 50°
TRAVERSE ON PLATFORM   360°
TRAVERSE OFF PLATFORM   16°
M.V.   890 m/s   2920 ft/sec
MAXIMUM RANGE   23,700 m   25,928 yards
SHELL WEIGHT   43 kg   94.8 lb

Krupp 15.2 cm Model 09 and 10

Among the many elderly pieces still in use with some Russian units in 1941 were two Krupp imports dating back to 1909 and 1910. These two filed howitzers were generally similar in appearance but differed in detail—for instance the 09 model was L/16 long and the 10 was L/15. By 1941 these two veterans were used only by reserve and other second line units and had almost passed from the scene but some were reported as captured by the Germans who did not take them into service but appear to have reduced them to scrap instead. Both guns were horse drawn conventional pieces with rather poor performance.

DATA (Model 10 Kp)
CALIBRE   152.4 mm   6 in
LENGTH OF PIECE (L/15)   2280 mm   90 in
WEIGHT TRAVELLING   2465 kg   5435 lb
WEIGHT IN ACTION   2175 kg   4796 lb
ELEVATION   —5° to 45°

TRAVERSE   5°
M.V.   350 m/s   1148 ft/sec
MAXIMUM RANGE   8200 m   8970 yards
SHELL WEIGHT   41 kg   90.4 lb

Krupp 15.2 cm Model 09

17 cm Kanone 18 in Morserlafette

The 17 cm K 18 in Mrs Laf entered service in 1941 **and** was intended to be the replacement for the larger 21 cm equipments and also for the various 15 cm guns that were inadequate for their task. It was a Krupp gun mounted on the carriage of the 21 cm Mrs 18. This carriage was unusual in having two separate recoil systems. One was the normal barrel recoil mechanism and the second was on the gun platform which slid back along rails mounted on the trail. In action the gun rested on this trail platform and could be easily rotated through 360° by one man. Despite the weapon's bulk it could be quickly brought into action with a minimum of external equipment. The K 18 soon proved itself to be a very good gun and was soon given a production priority over other guns of its type. Despite being produced in large numbers demand was always ahead of supply and many of the guns that the K 18 was intended to replace remained in use. American and British units often used captured examples themselves, especially during the 1944-1945 European campaign. The normal towing vehicle for this gun was usually the SdKfz 8 half-track.

DATA
CALIBRE   172.5 mm   6.79 in
LENGTH OF PIECE (L/50)   8529.5 mm   335.8 in
LENGTH OF BARREL   8103 mm   319 in
LENGTH OF RIFLING   6464 mm   254.5 in
WEIGHT IN ACTION   17,520 kg   38,632 lb
ELEVATION   0° to 50°
TRAVERSE (top carriage)   16°
TRAVERSE (total)   360°
M.V. (max)   925 m/s   3035 ft/sec
MAXIMUM RANGE   29,600 m   32,382 yards
SHELL WEIGHT (HE)   68 kg   149.9 lb
SHELL WEIGHT (long range HE)   62.8 kg   138.5 lb

langer 21 cm Morser

The lg 21 cm Mrs was placed into service in 1916 and was produced by Krupps. Designed primarily for static warfare it was transported in two loads but by 1939 the design had been revised for motor traction in one load. In its revised form the spoked wheels were replaced by solid rubber-tyred discs and the large shield was removed. Both the revised and original versions were in use during World War 2 but only the modernised model saw action in the field. The lg 21 cm Mrs was a large cumbersome weapon but it fired a very useful shell. It was eventually replaced by the 21 cm Mrs 18 and was then relegated to static defence positions.

DATA
CALIBRE   211 mm   8.3 in
LENGTH OF PIECE (L/14.6)   3063 mm   120.6 in
LENGTH OF BARREL   2675 mm   105.3 in
LENGTH OF RIFLING (L/10.88)   2296 mm   90.4 in
WEIGHT IN ACTION (late version)   9220 kg   20,330 lb
ELEVATION   6° to 70°
TRAVERSE   4°
M.V.   393 m/s   1289 ft/sec
MAXIMUM RANGE   11,100 m   12,143 yards
SHELL WEIGHT (HE)   113 kg   249.1 lb
SHELL WEIGHT (anti-concrete)   121.4 kg   267.7 lb

21 cm Morser 18

Along with the 17 cm K 18, the 21 cm Mrs 18 formed the backbone of the German heavy artillery. Both pieces shared the same design of dual-recoil carriage. The 21 cm Mrs 18 was another Krupp product and it entered service in 1939, but in 1942 production ceased in favour of the 17 cm K 18. However the Mrs 18 was used in some numbers and was encountered on all Fronts. A wide range of ammunition was developed for this howitzer including anti-concrete ammunition, a special muzzle stick bomb, and even a special 'Röchling' fin-stabilised shell. There were two main variants of the carriage—one used two solid rubber tyres and the later version had four pneumatic tyres. The 21 cm Mrs 18 design was so arranged that it could fire in either a low or a high register which with the variations possible using the six propelling charges meant that the piece could fire over a very wide band of ranges (minimum range was 3000 m—3280 yards).

DATA
CALIBRE   210.9 mm   8.3 in
LENGTH OF PIECE (L/31)   6510 mm   256.3 in
LENGTH OF BARREL   6070 mm   239.3 in
LENGTH OF RIFLING   5274 mm   207.6 in
WEIGHT IN ACTION   16,700 kg   36,824 lb
ELEVATION   0° to 70°
TRAVERS (top carriage)   16°
TRAVERSE (total)   360°
M.V. (max)   565 m/s   1854 ft/sec
MAXIMUM RANGE (HE)   16,700 m   18,270 yards
SHELL WEIGHT (HE)   121 kg   266.8 lb
SHELL WEIGHT (anti-concrete)   129.4 kg   285.3 lb

21 cm Kanone 38

In 1938 Krupps were asked to produce a new design of gun as a possible replacement for the 21 cm Mrs 18 which did not fully meet OKH requirements. The initial order was for fifteen guns to be delivered by 1940 but production was slow and only seven had been produced by 1943 and production then ceased. The new gun was the 21 cm K 38 and it has been acknowledged as one of the best designs of its class produced during World War 2. It embodied all the lessons learned with the Krupps 17 and 21 cm guns and used a refined version of the dual-recoil carriage. The whole gun could be emplaced using only hand-operated winches on the carriage, and large traverse corrections could be easily made. When travelling the gun was carried in two loads with a further vehicle carrying stores and accessories. One of these guns was sent to Japan but what use they made of it is unknown, and indeed it is not known if it even got there.

DATA
CALIBRE   210.9 mm   8.3 in
LENGTH OF PIECE (L/55.5)   11,620 mm   457.48 in
LENGTH OF BARREL   11,075 mm   436 in
LENGTH OF RIFLING   8717 mm   343.19 in
WEIGHT IN ACTION   25,300 kg   55,787 lb
ELEVATION   0° to 50°
TRAVERSE (top carriage)   17°
TRAVERSE (total)   360°
M.V.   905 m/s   2970 ft/sec
MAXIMUM RANGE   33,900 m   37,087 yards
SHELL WEIGHT (HE)   120 kg   265 lb

ITALY

Cannone da 149/35

DATA

CALIBRE   149.1 mm   5.87 in
LENGTH OF PIECE (L/38.7)   5722 mm
   225.3 in
LENGTH OF BARREL (L/36.6)   5464 mm
   215.15 in
LENGTH OF RIFLING (L/30.9)   4604 mm
   181.28 in
WEIGHT IN ACTION   8220 kg   18,125 lb
ELEVATION   —10° to 35°
TRAVERSE   0°
M.V. (max)   651 m/s   2136 ft/sec
MAXIMUM RANGE (approx)   16,500 m
   18,050 yards
SHELL WEIGHT (HE modello 32)   45.96 kg
   101.3 lb

One of the most ancient designs still in service with the Italian Army in 1940 was the Cannone da 149/35, or 149/35 A. The original 149/35 was an Armstrong barrel placed on a carriage without recoil or traversing mechanism in about 1900. All the recoil forces were absorbed by the carriage moving back up two ramps placed behind the wheels, and further movement was made difficult by strapping large flat plates round the wheel rims (these plates were also used when crossing soft ground). After each shot the piece had to be placed back into position and re-layed. All traversing movements were made by moving the carriage. By 1940 the 149/35 was obsolete and was intended for replacement by the 149/40 but this piece was never produced in sufficient quantities for this to happen. In June 1940 there were still 895 pieces on hand and these were used in Greece and Albania, and as late as 1942 there were still 64 in North Africa. There were various versions of the 149/35 with variations to the rifling and carriage, and one version was known as the 149/35 S. As a measure of the age of the 149/35 it can be mentioned that it continued to use a grapeshot projectile (Granate a pallette da 149/12/35), it was fired by a friction igniter, and it was laid by a sighting circle.

Cannone da 149/40 modello 35

The first prototype of a new 149 mm gun for the Italian Army was produced in 1934 by Ansaldo and the type was selected for service later as the modello 35. By 1940 orders had been made for a total of 590 but by the end of September only a few had been delivered—3 were in Italy, 12 in North Africa and 36 were in use in Russia with the Italian forces. The modello 35 was a good advanced design which rested off its wheels when fired. The large split trails retained the anomaly of hammered trail spikes for anchoring, but the wheels were kept in place when the gun fired to give a measure of stability. The modello 35 can be regarded as one of the best of the Italian designs but the small numbers produced could make no real contribution to the rather poor showing of the Italian artillery arm. On the road the modello 35 was towed in two loads by Breda tractors. In 1943 any that the Germans could lay hands on were pressed into their own use as the 15 cm K 408(i) and in April 1944 Ansaldo produced a further 12 for German use.

DATA
CALIBRE 149.1 mm 5.87 in
LENGTH OF PIECE (L/40.5) 6036 mm 237.66 in
LENGTH OF BARREL 5964 mm 234.8 in
LENGTH OF RIFLING 4965.6 mm 195.52 in
WEIGHT IN ACTION 11,340 kg 25,004 lb
ELEVATION 0° to 45°
TRAVERSE 60°
M.V. (max) 800 m/s 2625 ft/sec
MAXIMUM RANGE 23,700 m 25,928 yards
SHELL WEIGHT 46 kg 101.4 lb

Obice da 149/19 modello 37, 41 e 42

DATA (modello 37)
CALIBRE   149.1 mm   5.87 in
LENGTH OF PIECE (L/20.4)   3034 mm
   119.46 in
LENGTH OF BARREL (L/19)   2897 mm
   114 in
LENGTH OF RIFLING   2431.5 mm   95.74 in
WEIGHT TRAVELLING (complete)   6700 kg
   14,774 lb
WEIGHT IN ACTION   5500 kg   1,127 lb
ELEVATION   +5° to +60°
ELEVATION (modello 42)   −3° to +60°
TRAVERSE   50°
M.V.   597 m/s   1960 yards
MAXIMUM RANGE   14,250 m   15,590 yards
MAXIMUM RANGE (modello 42)   15,300 m
   16,738 yards
SHELL WEIGHT   42.55 kg   93.8 lb

Development of a new Italian 149 mm howitzer began in 1930 but it was not until 1938 that a series of experimental pieces produced by O.T.O. and Ansaldo under the auspices of the Direzione Servizio Tecnico Armi e Munizioni, bought about the first of the Obice da 149/19 series namely the modello 37. Sixteen of these pieces were produced and later a total of 1392 pieces were ordered from O.T.O. and Ansaldo. Production rates were low and by September 1942 only 147 had been made. By 1943 there were sufficient pieces to arm 24 artillery battalions (gruppi) but the full target total was never met. The three models, the 37, 41 and 42 differed only in detail, the construction and carriage were sound but unremarkable designs, and the type remained in service until 1951 with the Italian Army. The type also served with the Wehrmacht as the 15 cm sFH 404(i) and after 1943 was kept in production for the Germans alone. Despite its conventional design and split-trail carriage the 149/19 was thought of highly by the Italians who regarded it as a superior design to comparable Allied equipments.

Obice da 149/19 modello 41

Obice da 149/19 modello 37

Cannone da 152/45

DATA
CALIBRE   152.4 mm   6 in
LENGTH OF PIECE (L/46.7)   7138 mm   281 in
LENGTH OF BARREL   6898 mm   271.6 in
LENGTH OF RIFLING (L/36.6)   5570 mm
   219.3 in
WEIGHT IN ACTION   16,672 kg   36,762 lb
ELEVATION   −5° to 45°
TRAVERSE   10° or 60°
M.V. (max)   830 m/s   2723 ft/sec
MAXIMUM RANGE   19,400 m   21,223 yards
SHELL WEIGHT   47 kg   103.6 lb

The Cannone da 152/45 was another Italian World War 1 (1917) veteran still in use in 1940. The gun was originally a naval piece placed onto a heavy land carriage for long-range counter-battery work. Emplacing the 152/45 involved a great deal of time and labour as the firing platform had to be dug in and a pit dug under the breech if high elevation angles were to be used. In 1939 there were still 53 in use and these appear to have been used as home defence weapons, mainly in the North of Italy where they provided some measure of support for Alpine formations.

Cannone da 152/45

Mortaio da 210/8 D.S.

The 210/8 was a World War 1 piece still in use in 1940. It was intended originally as a siege mortar for the reduction of fixed defences and was thus not designed as a mobile gun and was fired from carefully prepared emplacements. During World War 2 it was not used outside Italy and was retained as a fortification and coastal defence weapon.

DATA
CALIBRE   210 mm   8.269 in
LENGTH OF PIECE (L/9.7)   2048 mm   80.64 in
LENGTH OF RIFLING (L/7.1)   1495 mm   58.86 in
WEIGHT IN ACTION   5500 kg   12,128 lb
ELEVATION   —15° to 70°
TRAVERSE (emplaced)   360°
M.V.   340 m/s   1115 ft/sec
MAXIMUM RANGE   8450 m   9244 yards
SHELL WEIGHT   101.5 kg   223.8 lb

Obice da 210/22 modello 35

The Obice da 210/22 was one of the two pieces selected during the late 1930s for the belated modernisation of the Italian Army heavy artillery (the other piece was the Cannone da 149/40). The design originated with the Servizio Tecnici Armi e Munizioni (STAM) and construction was carried out by Ansaldo, but later OTO was involved. A total of 346 were ordered by 1940 but production was so slow that in September 1942 only 20 were in service—5 in Italy and 15 in Russia. The 210/22 was one of the best of all the Italian designs as it was accurate, hard-hitting and mobile. The split-trail carriage was so arranged that the four road wheels were raised off the ground for firing and the carriage and platform could be traversed through 360° once the trail spades had been raised. On the road the 210/22 was carried in two loads but it could be further broken down into four loads with an extra load for extras and assembly equipment. After 1943 the Germans kept the 210/22 in production for their own use as the 21 cm H 520(i). Despite the urgent need of this piece by the Italians a number were sold to Hungary. To the Hungarians the type was known as the 21 cm 39.M. They found that in service the carriages would not stand up to prolonged use and began to incorporate their own changes to produce the 21 cm 40.M. At the same time they began to build their own pieces with all their own changes and their final version which was in production in 1943 was the 21 cm 40a.M.

DATA
CALIBRE   210 mm   8.269 in
LENGTH OF PIECE (L/23.8)   5000 mm   196.9 in
LENGTH OF RIFLING   4116.2 mm   162 in
WEIGHT IN ACTION   15,885 kg   35,026 lb
ELEVATION   0° to 70°
TRAVERSE   75°
M.V.   560 m/s   1837 ft/sec
MAXIMUM RANGE   15,407 m   16,855 yards
SHELL WEIGHT   101 or 133 kg   222.7 or 293 lb

modello 35 barrel on transporter

modello 35 carriage

JAPAN

150 mm Howitzer Type 38

In 1905 the Japanese Army started to equip itself with modern weapons and opened the Osaka Arsenal. One of the first weapons to be produced was a licence-built Krupp design that emerged as the Type 38. The design used a simple box trail, a hydro-spring recoil mechanism and a short barrel. By 1941 the design was obsolete but it still remained in use with some second-line and home defence units. After 1942 it was withdrawn from use.

150 mm Howitzer Type 4

As early as 1915 the shortcomings of the Type 38 Howitzer were becoming apparent and in that year the design of a new piece was started at Osaka Arsenal. The new design became the Type 4 and it remained the standard piece of its class until 1936. Even though it was due to be replaced by the later Type 96 it remained in widespread use throughout the Pacific and Chinese campaigns and as a result of the latter conflict the Type 4 became an integral part of the varied Chinese inventory. The Type 4 was a typical Japanese design being conventional but very light, so light in fact that the piece would not be moved far over rough ground in one load or the trail could break under the strain. As a result it was carried in two loads. The Type 4 was the first Japanese gun to use a hydropneumatic recoil system. This system enabled the gun to fire at extreme angles of elevation and the box trail could be adjusted to accommodate this angle. The same ammunition as used for the Type 38 was used and the separate cartridge case could accommodate up to five charge increments.

DATA
CALIBRE 149.2 mm 5.87 in
LENGTH OF PIECE (L/11) 1640 mm 64.5 in
WEIGHT IN ACTION 2250 kg 4960 lb
ELEVATION 0° to 42° 30′
TRAVERE 5°
M.V. 290 m/s 951 ft/sec
MAXIMUM RANGE 5900 m 6455 yards
SHELL WEIGHT 35.9 kg 79.16 lb

Self-propelled carriage
Self-propelled 15 cm Howitzer on Type 97 Medium Tank chassis

DATA
CALIBRE 149.2 mm 5.87 in
LENGTH OF BARREL (L/14.6) 2169 mm 85.4 in
LENGTH OF RIFLING 1524 mm 60 in
WEIGHT IN ACTION 2797 kg 6160 lb
ELEVATION (normal) —5° to 45°
ELEVATION (max) —5° to 65°
TRAVERSE 6°
M.V. 410 m/s 1345 ft/sec
MAXIMUM RANGE 9575 m 10,464 yards
SHELL WEIGHT 35.9 kg 79.16 lb

1

2

3

4

5

1,2,3,5. 150 mm Howitzer Type 4 **4.** *Type 4 in use by the Chinese Army*

150 mm Howitzer Type 96

The Type 96 was intended as the replacement weapon for the Type 4 and was first produced in 1936. Despite production in some numbers it never replaced the earlier howitzer but it was encountered on all fronts used by the Japanese. It was heavier than the earlier piece but could be towed in one load by a tractor. Range was increased and the Type 38 ammunition remained in use, albeit with some improvements.

DATA
CALIBRE   149.2 mm   5.87 in
LENGTH OF BARREL (L/23.37)   3505 mm   138 in
LENGTH OF RIFLING   2819 mm   111 in
WEIGHT TRAVELLING   4924 kg   10,846 lb
WEIGHT IN ACTION   4135 kg   9108 lb
ELEVATION (max)   —5° to 75°
TRAVERSE   30°
M.V. (max)   539 m/s   1768 ft/sec
MAXIMUM RANGE   11,870 m   12,971 yards
SHELL WEIGHT (old ammunition)   35.9 kg   79.16 lb
SHELL WEIGHT (new ammunition)   30.8 kg   67.9 lb

150 mm Howitzer Type 96

150 mm Gun Type 89

First produced at Osaka Arsenal in 1929 the Type 89 gun was not produced in large numbers but it formed the only viable component of the Japanese Army long-range artillery. It was transported in two loads and the time to get into action was excessively long when compared to similar weapons in service elsewhere. It was used in the early Philippine and Malaya campaigns but thereafter was withdrawn from use and used as a home defence weapon.

DATA
CALIBRE   149.1 mm   5.87 in
LENGTH OF BARREL (L/30)   4475 mm
    176 in
WEIGHT IN ACTION   10,409 kg   22,928.4 lb
ELEVATION   —5° to 43°
TRAVERSE   40°
M.V.   686 m/s   2250 ft/sec
MAXIMUM RANGE   19,950 m   21,800 yards
SHELL WEIGHT   45.9 kg   101.12 lb

NORWAY
Kongsberg 12 cm Model 1932

In 1932 a new field howitzer built and designed by the Norwegian Kongsberg Arsenal began to be issued to the three heavy artillery batteries of the Norwegian Army. This piece existed in two forms, one suitable for horse traction with wooden-spoked wheels and the other had rubber-rimmed steel wheels suitable for tractor towing. A shield was an extra. Very few of these howitzers had been built by 1939 and after 1940 these few were impressed into German use as the 12 cm leFH 376(n) and used by occupation units.

DATA
CALIBRE   120 mm   4.72 in
LENGTH OF PIECE (L/20)   2400 mm   94.5 in
LENGTH OF BORE (L/15.5)   1860 mm   73.2 in
WEIGHT IN ACTION (tractor)   1990 kg   4388 lb
ELEVATION   —5° to 43°
TRAVERSE   54°
M.V.   450 m/s   1476 ft/sec
MAXIMUM RANGE   10,300 m   11,268 yards
SHELL WEIGHT   20.4 kg   45 lb

SWEDEN
Bofors 12 cm M.14

In 1939 Holland still had a total of about 40 12 cm howitzers that had been bought direct from the Swedish firm of Bofors during World War 1. This piece was known as the Lichte Houwitzer 12 cm L 14 or 12 cm L 14 and was a conventional design with little to comment upon. It served alongside an essentially similar Krupp howitzer for many years but by 1940 the Krupp guns had been withdrawn leaving only the Bofors piece to provide a measure of light artillery support to the Dutch army. The type is mentioned in German records as the 12 cm leFH 373(h) but it does not appear to have been used by them.

DATA
CALIBRE   120 mm   4.725 in
LENGTH OF PIECE (L/14)   1725 mm   69.92 in
LENGTH OF BARREL   1420 mm   55.9 in
WEIGHT TRAVELLING   2520 kg   5556 lb
WEIGHT IN ACTION   1610 kg   3550 lb
ELEVATION   —4° 48′ to 43°
TRAVERSE   6°
M.V.   317 m/s   1040 ft/sec
MAXIMUM RANGE   6050 m   6618 yards
SHELL WEIGHT   16.5 kg   36.38 lb

UNITED KINGDOM
Q.F. 4.5 inch, Howitzer Mark 2

DATA

CALIBRE   114.3 mm   4.5 in
LENGTH OF PIECE (L/15.55)   1778 mm   70 in
LENGTH OF BARREL   1526.8 mm   60.11 in
LENGTH OF RIFLING   1343 mm   52.9 in
WEIGHT IN ACTION (Mark 1P)   1494 kg
   3291 lb
ELEVATION   —5° to 45°
TRAVERSE   6°
M.V. (max)   305 m/s   1000 ft/sec
MAXIMUM RANGE   6040 m   6600 yards
SHELL WEIGHT (HE)   15.66 kg   34.5 lb

The original 4.5 inch Howitzer Mark 1 first went to war in 1914 and as a result of experience was modified into the Mark 2 with some changes to the sliding breech block. After 1918 this piece was in service in large numbers as it had proved itself to be one of the most effective artillery weapons of World War 1. A committee had asked that it be replaced by a combined gun-howitzer design after investigations in 1925 (this eventually emerged as the 25 pr Mark 2) but the large stocks on hand during the 1920s and 1930s meant that in 1939 the 4.5 inch howitzer was still in widespread service in the British Army. In that year most of the older spoked wheel carriages, the Mark 1, had been converted into the Marks 1PA and 1R, both with pneumatic tyres and the piece was used with the Trailer Artillery No. 26 Mark 1. In this form the 4.5 inch Howitzer went with the BEF to France and fought its last major campaign in 1940. As a result of that campaign the Germans captured 96 4.5 inch howitzers and pressed them into use as the 11.4 cm leFH 361(e) and many were emplaced in the Atlantic Wall defences. Back in the UK the 4.5 continued in use as a training gun and in the absence of anything else it continued in service during the early Desert battles and saw action in Somaliland and Eritrea. It was not until 1944 that the last 4.5 was withdrawn from service but by then it was used only in the training role.

As well as being one of the major equipments of the British Field Regiments in 1939 the 4.5 inch Howitzer also equipped many Commonwealth and colonial armies. Some were also supplied to Rumania and Eire while a small number ended up in Poland—most of these were the version using the original Mark 1 horse-drawn carriage. Russia also obtained a number but from what source is uncertain—it may be that these were captured in 1921 during the Russian Civil War from the White Russian forces. By 1941 these had been updated by the use of pneumatic tyres and eventually came under the German fold as the 11.5 cm leFH 362(r)—note the change in calibre from the 'British' designation. Only small numbers of these Russian trophies appear to have been used by the Germans.

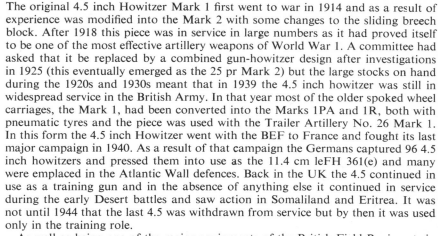

4.5 inch Howitzer Mark 2 on Carriage 4.5 inch Howitzer Mk 1PA

4.5 inch Gun Mark I on Carriage 60 pr Mark IV and IVP

During the mid-1930s the need to update and re-equip the medium artillery regiments of the Royal Artillery was becoming an urgent priority, but funds for new equipments were very low. In an attempt to provide some form of modern gun a total of 76 60 pr carriages were converted to take a new 4.5 inch barrel, and the carriages were further revised to be fitted with pneumatic wheels and modern brakes. The first conversions were made in 1937 and the first equipment was ready for service in 1938. The conversion did all it was required to do but the Director of Artillery asked for a more modern gun to follow and this eventually became the B.L. 4.5 inch Gun Mark 2. But in 1939 the 4.5 inch Gun Mark I was one of the better medium guns that the BEF took to France. In 1940 they had a total of 32 in use in France and the majority of these were either rendered useless or fell into German hands—none of the total of 32 returned to the UK. In German service the 4.5 inch Gun Mark 1 became the 11.4 cm K 365(e) and it was used both as a field piece and coastal defence gun but after about 1941 most were emplaced in the Atlantic Wall. In the UK most of the Mark 1 guns were used for training purposes and some saw action during the early Western Desert battles.

DATA
CALIBRE   114.3 mm   4.5 in
LENGTH OF PIECE (L/42.8)   4881 mm   192.19 in
LENGTH OF BARREL   4748.2 mm   186.96 in
LENGTH OF RIFLING   3977.8 mm   156.625 in
WEIGHT TRAVELLING   7250 kg   15,986 lb
WEIGHT IN ACTION   5730 kg   12,635 lb
ELEVATION   0° to 42°
TRAVERSE   7°
M.V.   686 m/s   2250 ft/sec
MAXIMUM RANGE   19,200 m   21,000 yards
SHELL WEIGHT   24.95 kg   55 lb

1

2

3

1,2,3. 4.5 inch Gun Mark 1 on Carriage 60 pr Mark 1VP

B.L. 4.5 inch Gun Mark 2 on Carriage 4.5 inch Gun Marks 1 and 2

DATA
CALIBRE 114.3 mm 4.5 in
LENGTH OF PIECE (L/43) 4896 mm 192.75 in
LENGTH OF BARREL 4763.8 mm 187.55 in
LENGTH OF RIFLING 3983 mm 156.825 in
WEIGHT TRAVELLING (shipping) 15,254 kg 33,600 lb
WEIGHT IN ACTION 5847 kg 12,880 lb
ELEVATION —5° to 45°
TRAVERSE 60°
M.V. (max) 686 m/s 2250 ft/sec
MAXIMUM RANGE 18,758 m 20,500 yards
SHELL WEIGHT 24.97 kg 55 lb
WEIGHT OF HE FILLING 1.76 kg 3.875 lb

During the late 1930s when it was realised that the 4.5 inch/60 pr conversion would not meet all the future requirements of the Royal Artillery Medium Regiments, the Director of Artillery proposed that a new design of 4.5 inch gun that could use the same carriage as the projected 5.5 inch howitzer. The gun design was developed and built by 1940 but difficulties with the new carriage held up production so that it was not until 1941 that the first new equipments reached the field. In service the 4.5 inch Gun Mark 2 was used for long-range counter-battery and interdiction fire but its use was hampered by the relatively low HE filling of the projectile. Thus the production priorities swung to the 5.5 inch Howitzer and the 4.5 inch Gun was withdrawn from service soon after hostilities ended in 1945. The gun itself was conventionally and sturdily constructed and the two Marks of carriage used differed only in detail. Both used split trails with prominent equilibriators.

1,2. Ordnance B.L. 4.5 inch Mark 11 on Carriage 4.5 inch Gun Mark 1

B.L. 60 pr Marks II and II*

DATA
CALIBRE 127 mm 5 in
LENGTH OF PIECE (L/38.45) 4883 mm 192.25 in
LENGTH OF BARREL 4699 mm 185 in
LENGTH OF RIFLING 4088.6 mm 160.968 in
WEIGHT TRAVELLING 6423 kg 14,148 lb
WEIGHT IN ACTION 5470 kg 12,048 lb
ELEVATION —4° 50′ to 35°
TRAVERSE 8°
M.V. (max) 667 m/s 2176 ft/sec
MAXIMUM RANGE 13,816 m 15,100 yards
SHELL WEIGHT 27.24 kg 60 lb

The original 60 pr gun was produced at the Elswick Ordnance Company works before 1914 and as the Mark I through to I** saw extensive action during World War 1, After 1918 the gun was further modified up to Mark II standard and further small changes produced the Mark II*. At the same time the early carriages were revised and updated to produce the Mark IV, IVP and IVR carriages. The Mark IV was a box trail carriage with spoked metal wheels while the Marks IVP and IVR had pneumatic wheels and suitable brakes. On the move the lengthy 60 pr barrel was drawn back to lay over the trail and the trail was supported on a two-wheeled limber. By 1939 most of the 60 pr carriages had been updated to Mark IVP or IVR standard. When the BEF went to France the elderly 60 pr made up the rump of the equipment of the Medium Regiments as there were only 16 of them in use with three reserves. All of these were lost during the 1940 campaigns and came under the arm of the Wehrmacht as the 12.7 cm K 382(e) but they were little used and seem to have been reduced to scrap. The remaining 60 prs that the British Army possessed saw some action in North Africa and Eritrea but after 1941 the type was withdrawn from use and lintered on only as a training and proofing gun. The United States had a few 60 prs still in reserve in 1941 which had the designation of 5 inch Gun M1918 but they were used as training guns only. In 1940, twelve of these American guns were sold to Brazil and they remained in use until at least the late 1960s.

60 pr Mark 11 on Mark 1VR Carriage

60 pr Mark 11 in the Western Desert, late 1940

60 pr Mark 11* on Mark 111 Carriage

60 pr being used for training in the North of England 1940

B.L. 5.5 inch Mark III Gun on Carriage 5.5 inch Marks I and II

The piece that was to become the 5.5 inch gun had its origins in the mid 1930s when a specification was issued for a 5 inch gun capable of firing a 100 lb shell to a range of 16,000 yards. In 1939 this was changed to a gun of 5.5 inches in calibre and the first pilot models were built and proofed in 1940. The proposed carriage proved to be too weak for the new 5.5 inch barrel as it had been built for a 5 inch piece and the necessary redesign held up production so that the first 5.5 inch guns entered service in 1941. Once in service they soon proved to be a most popular and useful weapon, so much so that they are still in use in 1975. In time they proved to be more useful than the 4.5 inch gun which used the same carriage as it had a much heavier and more destructive shell. Although the 5.5 inch Gun was referred to as a gun it was more often used as a howitzer and on the Continent was often referred to in reports as a gun-howitzer. The two Marks of trail differed only in detail.

DATA
CALIBRE   139.7 mm   5.5 in
LENGTH OF PIECE (L/31.2)   4358.6 mm
   171.6 in
LENGTH OF BARREL   4175.7 mm   164.4 in
LENGTH OF RIFLING   3437 mm   135.32 in
WEIGHT OF GUN AND CARRIAGE   5796 kg
   12,768 lb
ELEVATION   —5° to 45°
TRAVERSE   60°
M.V. (max)   760 m/s   1675 ft/sec
MAXIMUM RANGE   14,823 m   16,200 yards
SHELL WEIGHT   (light)   36.32 kg   80 lb
SHELL WEIGHT (normal)   45.4 kg   100 lb

1

2

3

1,2. Ordnance B.L. 5.5 inch Mark 111 on Carriage 5.5 inch Mark 1   3. 5.5 inch gun in the Western Desert

42

B.L. 6 inch Mark VIII Gun

DATA
CALIBRE 152.4 mm 6 in
LENGTH OF PIECE (L/36.6) 5580 mm
  219.7 in
WEIGHT IN ACTION 11,000 kg 24,255 lb
ELEVATION 0° to 38°
TRAVERSE 8°
M.V. 770 m/s 2526 ft/sec
MAXIMUM RANGE 16,600 m 18,160 yards
SHELL WEIGHT 45.4 kg 100 lb

The 6 inch Mark VIII gun only just manages to merit a mention in these pages for it was a World War 1 improvisation brought about by mounting a coast defence/naval gun barrel onto the 8 inch Howitzer carriage. As such it saw limited service during World War 1, and was thus ready to hand when the United States entered the conflict in 1917. At that time the US Army was desperately short of heavy artillery and took on large numbers of these guns for use in France. After 1918 most of these were shipped to Panama where they were used as coastal defence guns using the concrete 'Panama Mount' platforms. By 1939, even the addition of pneumatic-tyred carriages could not disguise the fact that these guns were obsolete and they were about to be scrapped when war broke out in Europe. At this juncture Brazil felt a need for some form of coastal defence weapon and 99 were brought by them direct from the Panama Canal defences. These pieces remained in use until at least the late 1960s at various points round the coast of Brazil. The American designation was 6 inch Gun M1917.

6 inch Gun M1917 in use with the Brazilian Army, 1943

B.L. 6 inch Mark XIX Gun on Marks VIII and VIIIA Travelling Carriages

The first 6 inch Land Service guns had their origins as long range bombardment pieces during World War 1. They had a long and tortuous development history which is outside the scope of this book, but suffice it to say that in 1939 only the Mark XIX gun was in first-line service. Originally this used the carriage developed for the 8 inch Howitzer, complete with large engine wheels, but by 1939 some of these carriages had been updated by the use of pneumatic-tyred wheels and other changes. Very few of these elderly guns had been so converted for the climate of opinion current during the 1930s was that aircraft could carry out most of the tasks carried out by heavy artillery in days gone by, and anyway, defence funds were very small. Thus the BEF in France in 1940 found itself with only 12 6 inch guns in the line with a single piece held in reserve. Most of these found their way into German hands and none were bought back across the Channel. The Germans did not add this piece to their inventory and it would seem that the small number that remained were reduced to scrap. Back in the UK a number of Mark XIX guns were emplaced for Home Defence.

DATA
CALIBRE 152.4 mm 6 in
LENGTH OF PIECE (L/36.5) 5568 mm
  219.22 in
LENGTH OF BARREL (L/35) 5334 mm
  210 in
LENGTH OF RIFLING 4337.25 mm
  170.758 in
WEIGHT TRAVELLING 10,348 kg 22,792 lb
ELEVATION 0° to 38°
TRAVERSE 8°
M.V. (max) 733 m/s 2405 ft/sec
MAXIMUM RANGE 17,156 m 18,750 yards
SHELL WEIGHT (approx) 45.4 kg 100 lb

B.L. 6 inch Gun Mark XIX on Mark VIII Carriage

6 inch Mark XIX Gun with Carriage on pneumatic tyres

A Mark XIX Gun being used for coast defence in Southern England, 1942

B.L. 6 inch 26 cwt Howitzer Mark I on Carriages Marks 1P and 1R

The design of that 6 inch cwt Howitzer began in 1915 and the first pieces reached the field in the same year. It was produced in large numbers and by the end of the war there were over 4000 in use. Throughout the life of this piece few modifications were made and the carriage was little changed until the late 1930s when the Marks 1P and 1R carriages were introduced, both with pneumatic tyres and suitable brakes. In 1939 the 6 inch Howitzer made up the largest single component of the Medium Regiments of the BEF for in France there were 176 serving with the batteries and a further 45 held in reserve. Most of these fell into German hands when they became an important part of the Wehrmacht inventory as the 15.2 cm sFH 412(e). The remaining guns in the UK were used for home defence and training and in 1941 some were still in action in the Western Desert and in Eritrea. That was their last major campaign for after 1941 they were gradually withdrawn from service and became officially obsolete in 1945.

After 1918 many 6 inch Howitzers were exported to other countries. Russia obtained a batch but by 1941 these appear to have been withdrawn from use. Below is a short list of the main user states in 1939 along with the eventual German designation.

Belgium: Obusier de 6″   *15.2 cm sFH 410(b)*
Holland: Houwitzer 6″   *15.2 cm sFH 407(h)*
Italy: Obice da 152/13   *15.2 cm sFH 412(i)*

DATA
CALIBRE   152.4 mm   6 in
LENGTH OF PIECE (L/14.6)   2223 mm 87.55 in
LENGTH OF BARREL (L/13.3)   2027 mm 79.8 in
LENGTH OF RIFLING   1637.6 mm   64.475 in
WEIGHT TRAVELLING (Mark 1R)   4471 kg 9849 lb
ELEVATION   0° to 45°
TRAVERSE   8°
M.V. (max)   429 m/s   1409 ft/sec
MAXIMUM RANGE   10,430 m   11,400 yards
SHELL WEIGHT   45.48 kg   100.19 lb

1

1,2,4. *6 inch 26 cwt Howitzer Mark I on Carriage Mark 1P* **3.** *A WW1 60 pr in use for training in the UK in July 1940—note the muzzle tampion is still fitted* **5.** *60 pr howitzers still in use on their Mark I carriages in early 1940* **6.** *Dutch Howitzer 6 inch* **7.** *Italian Obice da 152/13* **8.** *60 pr Howitzer in action in North Africa*

45

B.L. 7.2 inch Howitzer Marks I to V on Carriage 7.2 inch Howitzer Mark I

During the early 1930s the need for modern heavy artillery was felt to be a thing of the past as the airplane was deemed suitable to carry out many of its tasks. By about 1935 this point of view began to change and a new range of heavy artillery was proposed but defence funds were small and development was very slow. Two projects were for a 6.85 inch gun and a 7.85 inch howitzer but both were dropped in 1939 in favour of a new 9.2 inch howitzer but this project was dropped during 1940. Thus in 1940, after Dunkirk, the British Army was left with virtually no modern heavy guns. As an expedient a number of 8 inch Howitzer barrels were rebored and relined with a new 7.2 inch liner to produce the 7.2 inch Howitzer. The result was meant only as a stop-gap but in the field it was soon found to be a most useful weapon and demands for more were soon made by field units. Despite its success as a weapon it had a definite disadvantage for the gunners who had to serve the weapon. The carriage of the 8 inch Howitzer was retained and fitted with large balloon tyres. When fired, the 7.2 inch Howitzer recoil forces were too heavy for the carriage mechanism and ramps had to be placed behind the wheels for the piece to run up after firing. The piece then ran down to its former position and then had to be re-layed. On occasion the gun would run over the top of these wooden ramps and then had to be man-handled back into position. There were several Marks of barrel, the Marks I, I*, II, III, IV and V and they differed only in the origins of the barrel as several different Marks of 8 inch barrel were used (the Mark I* was a re-lined Mark 1 barrel). The Marks II to V were relined American barrels originally produced during World War 1. The 7.2 inch Howitzer entered service in 1941 and thereafter served on most fronts until 1945.

DATA

CALIBRE 182.9 mm 7.2 in
LENGTH OF PIECE (L/23.7) 4343 mm 171 in
LENGTH OF BARREL 4092 mm 161.1 in
LENGTH OF RIFLING 3258mm 128.28 in
WEIGHT TRAVELLING (Mark 1& 4)
  10,397 kg 22,900 lb
ELEVATION 0° to 45°
TRAVERSE 8°
M.V. (max) 518 m/s 1700 ft/sec
MAXIMUM RANGE 15,464 m 16,900 yards
SHELL WEIGHT 91.7 kg 202 lb

1

2

3

1,2. 7.2 inch Howitzer on Mark I Carriage
3. 7.2 inch Howitzer in action, N.W. Europe,
September, 1944

B.L. 7.2 inch Howitzer Mark 6 on Carriage 155 mm/8 inch Howitzer M1

DATA
CALIBRE   182.9 mm   7.2 in
LENGTH OF PIECE (L/34.4)   6300 mm   248 in
WEIGHT IN ACTION (approx)   13,220 kg
   29,120 lb
ELEVATION   —2° to 65°
TRAVERSE   60°
M.V.   497 m/s   1630 ft/sec
MAXIMUM RANGE   17,995m 19,667 yards
SHELL WEIGHT   91.7 kg   202 lb

Despite the success of the projectile fired by the 7.2 inch Howitzer Marks I to V it had to be admitted that the carriage used for the barrel was unstable and unsatisfactory. In 1944 a longer development of the 7.2 inch barrel, the Mark 6, was fitted to the American 155 mm/8 inch Howitzer M1 carriage and the result was a definite improvement in stability, range and accuracy. As a result the earlier field carriages were gradually withdrawn as the longer barrel on the American carriage became available, and the combination served on for many years after the war. Small numbers of Marks 1 and 1* barrels were fitted to the American carriage as the Marks 5* and the Mark 6/1 barrel was a repaired Mark 6 barrel.

B.L. 8 inch Howitzer Mark VIII on Mark VIIA and VIIAP Carriages

The original Mark VIII Howitzer had its origins in the Mark VII which was introduced into British service in late 1916. Over the years most of the early Mark VII pieces were converted to Mark VIII standards and during the late 1930s the original carriage with large traction engine wheels was converted to more modern standards with the addition of pneumatic tyres—this carriage was also used by the 6 inch Gun. The BEF took one Heavy Regiment to France which was equipped with twelve 8 inch Howitzers plus one reserve piece, but in 1940 most of these fell intact into German hands. These howitzers then became the 20.3 cm sH 501(e) but they were little used by the Germans and by 1944 they had been scrapped. Back in the UK, the remaining 8 inch Howitzers were used for home defence and training and the barrels were gradually converted to become 7.2 inch Howitzer barrels so that by 1944 the 8 inch Howitzer had passed from the scene.

In the United States the 8 inch Howitzer had been placed in production to meet a British order in 1916 and in 1917 the Midvale Steel Co. was ordered to continue production for the US Army To the Americans the 8 inch Howitzer became the 8 inch Howitzer M1917 and in 1941 there were still large numbers (about 200) scattered around the United States and overseas bases. They were gradually withdrawn from use and the barrels were renovated and placed on more modern carriages. Many of the British 7.2 inch Howitzers used barrels that had originally been produced on American production lines.

1,2,3. 8 inch Howitzer Mark VIII on Carriage Mark VIIAP

DATA
CALIPRE   203 mm   8 in   WEIGHT TRAVELLING   9101 kg   20,048 lb
LENGTH OF BIECE (L/18.5)   3767 mm   ELEVATION   0° to 45°
   148.3 in   TRAVERSE   8°
LENGTH OF BARREL   (L/17.3)   3515 mm   M.V.   457 m/s   1500 ft/sec
   138.4 in   MAXIMUM RANGE   11,346 m   12,400 yards
LENGTH OF RIFLING   2527.8 mm   99.52 in   SHELL WEIGHT   90.8 kg   200 lb

USA
4.5 inch Gun M1—Carriage M1A1

In 1939 the American Ordnance Department took stock of their existing equipment and decided to go ahead with the design of two new pieces, namely a 4.7 inch gun and a 155 mm howitzer, both of which would use the same carriage. Later it was decided that the 4.7 inch gun should be changed to 4.5 inch calibre in order that British ammunition could be used and American ammunition could be used by British units. The result was the 4.5 inch Gun M1. In service the M1 was found to have a valuable range but the HE content of the shell was found to be too small for the efforts involved and as soon as the war ended the type was withdrawn from use. The Carriage M1A1 differed from the M1 only in having electric brakes in place of the M1's air brakes. Up to 1945 426 M1 Guns were produced along with 1,969,000 projectiles.

DATA
CALIBRE 114.3 mm 4.5 in
LENGTH OF PIECE 4919.7 mm 193.69 in
LENGTH OF BORE (L/42) 4800 mm 189 in
LENGTH OF RIFLING 3982.7 mm 156.8 in
WEIGHT TRAVELLING 5654 kg 12,455 lb
ELEVATION 0° to 60°
TRAVERSE 53°
M.V. (max) 694 m/s 2275 ft/sec
MAXIMUM RANGE 23,529 m 25,715 yards
SHELL WEIGHT 24.92 kg 54.9 lb
WEIGHT OF HE FILLING 2,038 kg 4.49 lb

1

2

3

1-4. *4.5 inch Gun M1—Carriage M1*

4

48

155 mm Howitzer M1918—Carriage M1918A3

DATA

CALIBRE 155 mm 6.1 in
LENGTH OF PIECE 2332 mm 91.81 in
LENGTH OF BORE (L/13.64) 2114 mm
  83.246 in
LENGTH OF RIFLING 1737 mm 68.39 in
WEIGHT TRAVELLING 4321 kg 9518 lb
WEIGHT IN ACTION 3715 kg 8184 lb
ELEVATION 0° to 42° 20′
TRAVERSE 6°
M.V. (max) 451 m/s 1478 ft/sec
MAXIMUM RANGE 11,250 m 12,295 yards
SHELL WEIGHT (HE M102) 42.8 kg
  94.27 lb

1,2. 155 mm Howitzer M1918—Carriage M1918A3 3. British troops manning a 155 mm Howitzer M1918 in North Africa 4. An American-trained Chinese crew manning a M1918 in Burma 5. M1918 howitzers in action

In 1917 the American contingent in France took over large numbers of French C 17 S 155 mm howitzers and used them as the 155 mm Howitzer M1917 and M19171A. The type was selected for production in the United States and this American version then became the 155 mm Howitzer M1918 and differed from the French original in using a different breech mechanism. In June 1940 there were 2971 155 mm howitzers still in service with the US Army (this total included a number of M1917 pieces) of which 599 had been 'high-speeded'. This term referred to the result of experiments begun in 1933 to enable field pieces to be towed at high speeds behind modern tractors. For the 155 mm Howitzer the result was the Carriage M1918A3 which used pneumatic tyres and special wheel bearings. After 1940 the Howitzer M1918 and M1917 was scheduled for replacement by the 155 mm Howitzer M1 but the type remained in service for years. In the USA it was used as a coastal and training gun, but it saw extensive service in the Philippines and Far East campaigns, and was also used in Sicily and Italy. As it was still a viable weapon even after 1943 it was passed on to such Allies as China, and in Italy a number were used by the British Army for a period. Many were passed on to South American states—in 1943 four were given to Brazil and these remained in use until at least 1964. South African units used this piece in North Africa and Italy.

1

2

3

4

5

155 mm Howitzer M1 and M1A1—Carriage M1

The design and development of the 155 mm Howitzer M1 began in 1939 and was carried out by the Rock Island Arsenal. It was intended to use the same carriage as that intended for the 4.5 inch Gun M1, but as things turned out the howitzer was produced in far larger numbers than the gun. The M1 was first issued in 1942 and by 1945, 4035 had been produced. It was a very successful and popular weapon and soon gained itself a reputation for accuracy—a measure of its success is that in 1975 it is still in widespread service. The design of the howitzer was conventional and the split trail Carriage M1 used a firing jack under the wheel axle. Later versions of the carriage were the M1A1 and M1A2 which used different types of firing jack. A later version of the howitzer itself was the M1A1 which was constructed from a stronger grade steel. After the war the M1 was redesignated the 155 mm Howitzer M-114.

DATA
CALIBRE   155 mm   6.1 in
LENGTH OF PIECE   3810 mm   150 in
LENGTH OF BORE (L/20)   3100 mm   122 in
WEIGHT OF GUN AND CARRIAGE   5432 kg
   11,966 lb
ELEVATION   —2° to 65°
TRAVERSE   53°
M.V. (max)   564 m/s   1850 ft/sec
MAXIMUM RANGE   14,640 m   16,000 yards
SHELL WEIGHT (HE M107)   43.14 kg   95 lb
Self propelled Carriages
T64E1 Howitzer Motor Carriage—later
   M41 (Gorilla)

1

2

3

4

1-4. *155 mm Howitzer M1*

155 mm Gun M1917 and M1918M1—Carriage M3

DATA

CALIBRE   155 mm   6.1 in
LENGTH OF PIECE   5915 mm   232.87 in
LENGTH OF BORE (L/36.4)   5642 mm
   222.15 in
LENGTH OF RIFLING   4623 mm   182 in
WEIGHT TRAVELLING   11,600 kg   25,550 lb
WEIGHT IN ACTION (approx)   9125 kg
   20,100 lb
M.V. (AP M112)   720 m/s   2360 ft/sec
MAXIMUM RANGE   18,391 m   20,100 yards
SHELL WEIGHT (HE M101)   43 kg   94.71 lb
ELEVATION   0° to 35°
TRAVERSE   60°

Self-propelled Carriages
T6 Gun Motor Carriage—later M12

The 155 mm Gun M1917 was originally the French 155 mm GPF gun taken over by the US Army in France in 1917 and 1918. The type was selected for manufacture in the United States as the M1918M1 and was virtually identical to the original French gun, so much so that if an American breech block was fitted to a French gun the two were compatible and a gun so fitted was redesignated M1917A1. Over the years the carriages were progressively modified from the original Carriages M1917 and 1918 to the improved M1917A1 and M1918A1. Then came the Carriages M2 and M3 which were high speed carriages with pneumatic tyres and air brakes. These latter carriages were designed for the high speed deployment of 155 mm guns as coastal artillery round the coasts of the United States. As the entire seaboard could not be fortified special concrete platforms known as Panama Mounts were built at likely spots and the guns could then be rushed to any threatened point in an emergency. Despite their age the 155 mm guns were used widely during World War 2 both as coastal pieces and as field guns. They were used extensively during the Sicilian and Italian campaigns.

1

2

1,2. *155 mm Gun M1917A1—Carriage M2*
3. *155 mm Gun M1918M1—Carriage M3*
4. *155 mm M1918M1 guns in service with the First French Army in Alsace, 1944*

3

4

5

6

5,6. *155 mm Gun M1A1—Carriage M1* **7.** *A 155 mm Gun M1A1 on the island of Keiae Saima prior to the Invasion of Okinawa, March 1945* **8.** *A M1A1 in action with British troops against Gothic Line positions in Italy, 1944*

7

8

8 inch Howitzer M1—Carriage M1

DATA
CALIBRE   203.2 mm   8 in
LENGTH OF PIECE   5323 mm   209.59 in
LENGTH OF BORE (L/25)   5080 mm   200 in
WEIGHT TRAVELLING   14,515 kg   32,005 lb
WEIGHT IN ACTION   13,471 kg   29,703 lb
ELEVATION   —2° to 64°
TRAVERSE   60°
M.V. (max)   595 m/s   1950 ft/sec
MAXIMUM RANGE   16,937 m   18,510 yard
SHELL WEIGHT (M106)   90.8 kg   200 lb
Self-propelled Carriages
T83 Howitzer Motor Carriage—later M43

Like the 155 mm Gun M1, the 8 inch Howitzer M1 was developed from an existing design, in this case that of the British 8 inch Howitzer Marks VI to VIII which were issued to American forces in Europe in 1917-1918. Some of these pieces were built in the United States but by 1940 they were being phased out of service in favour of a new design based on the old 8 inch which was under development by the Hughes Tool Company. The new design known as the M1 entered service in 1942 and used the same carriage and breech mechanism as the 155 mm Gun M1. By 1945 1006 had been produced and after the war the type was redesignated the 8 inch Howitzer M-115. Throughout its service life the M1 gained for itself a reputation for accuracy and as a long range anti-fortification piece it was an excellent weapon.

8 inch Gun M1—Carriage M2

The need to replace existing long range bombardment weapons serving with the US Army was first recognised by the Calibre Board in 1919 but all work on the project was dropped in 1924. In 1939 the project was resumed and the first 8 inch Gun T2, later to be known as the M1, was approved in 1941. This 8 inch gun was designed to use the same carriage as a complementary 240 mm howitzer, the 240 mm Howitzer M1, but some changes had to be made to suit the 8 inch gun so the howitzer carriage became the Carriage M1 and gun carriage the M2. The 8 inch gun went into service in 1942 and it was a large, heavy and expensive weapon. On the move the gun was carried on a transport wagon and the piece had to be assembled using a mobile 20 ton crane mounted on a truck. The huge split trail was also carried on a special waggon. The towing vehicles were usually converted M3 Medium Tanks. Once in action the M1 had a rate of fire of one round a minute but after about ten minutes this had usually fallen to one round every two minutes. By 1945 139 had been produced. During the latter stages of the war this gun was issued to the 4th Super Heavy Battery (Royal Artillery) as the 8-inch Gun Mark 1.

DATA   203.2 mm   8 in
LENGTH OF PIECE   10,401 mm   409.5 in
LENGTH OF BORE (L/50) 10,160 mm   400 in
LENGTH OF RIFLING   8600 mm   338.6 in
WEIGHT COMPLETE   31,462 kg   69,300 lb
ELEVATION   —10° to 50°
TRAVERSE   40°
M.V.   900 m/s   2950 ft/sec
MAXIMUM RANGE (approx)   32,025 m   35,000 yards
SHELL WEIGHT (HE M103)   109.13 kg   240.37 lb

USSR

107 mm Field Gun Model 1910/30r

DATA
CALIBRE 106.7 mm 4.2 in
LENGTH OF PIECE (L/38) 4054 mm
  159.6 in
LENGTH OF RIFLING (L/31) 3314 mm
  130.47 in
WEIGHT TRAVELLING 2580 kg 5689lb
WEIGHT IN ACTION 2380 kg 5248 lb
ELEVATION —5° to 37°
TRAVERSE 6°
M.V. 670 m/s 2198 ft/sec
MAXIMUM RANGE 16,350 m 17,887 yards
SHELL WEIGHT 17.18 kg 37.88 lb

In 1930 it was decided that the elderly 107 mm Schneider guns needed updating and this was accomplished by placing a new and longer barrel onto the existing carriage. The result was the Model 1910/30, more usually known as the 107-10/30. It remained a horse-drawn gun, and it equipped many of the front-line artillery units in 1941 when the Germans invaded Russia. In the ensuing campaigns large numbers fell into German hands and these were used against their former owners as the 10.7 cm K 352(r). These captured guns were used not only in Russia but also as coast defence guns in the Atlantic Wall.

107 mm Field Gun Model 1940 M60

DATA
CALIBRE 106.7 mm 4.2 in
LENGTH OF PIECE (L/43.5) 4650.6 mm
  183.09 in
LENGTH OF BARREL 4465.4 mm 175.8 in
LENGTH OF RIFLING 3665.4 mm 144.3 in
WEIGHT TRAVELLING 4285 kg 9448 lb
WEIGHT IN ACTION (no shield) 3957 kg
  8725 lb
ELEVATION —6° 20′ to 43° 40′
TRAVERSE 60°
M.V. 720 m/s 2362 ft/sec
MAXIMUM RANGE 17,450 m 19,090 yards
SHELL WEIGHT 17.18 kg 37.88 lb

The 107 mm Field Gun Model 1940 was just entering service with the Russian Army when the Germans invaded in 1941. Its production was thus cut short just as large numbers were coming off the production lines, for the Germans captured many of the production facilities during their massive advances of 1941 and 1942. At the same time the Russian Army decided to concentrate on heavier calibres and so the 107 mm production lines were stopped. Relatively few of the Model 1940 guns actually saw service. As an indication of this, the Germans gave the piece the reporting designation of s.10.7 cm K 353(r), but there are no records of this model in German service despite the use of the earlier Model 1910/30. The Model 1940, usually known as the 107-40 M60, used the same carriage and wheels as the 152 mm Howitzer Model 1938, and a shield was an optional extra. It was designed to be tractor-towed in one load. At one time it was intended that this gun would be the main armament of the KV-1 and JS-1 tanks.

122 mm Field Gun Model 1931

The 122 mm Model 1931 field gun was an original Russian design introduced in 1931 to update the ageing heavy artillery inventory of the Russian Army. As with so many Russian guns, a new barrel was grafted onto an existing carriage, in this case that of the 152 mm Gun-howitzer Model 1934 which was introduced into service around the same time. The Model 1931, usually known as the 122-31, was a conventional and effective piece which was later considered good enough to add to the German armoury after the invasion of 1941. They used it as the 12.2 cm K 390/1(r), and even went to the extent of carrying large numbers of them across Europe to incorporate them into the Atlantic Wall defences.

DATA
CALIBRE 121.92 mm 4.8 in
LENGTH OF PIECE (L/46.34) 5650 mm 222.44 in
LENGTH OF BARREL 5483 mm 215.86 in
LENGTH OF RIFLING (L/37.7) 4600 mm 181.125 in
WEIGHT TRAVELLING 7800 kg 17,199 lb
WEIGHT IN ACTION 7100 kg 15,656 lb
ELEVATION —4° to 45°
TRAVERSE 56°
M.V. 800 m/s 2625 ft/sec
MAXIMUM RANGE 20,870 m 22,832 yards
SHELL WEIGHT 25 kg 55.125 lb

122 mm Field Gun Model 1931/37 (A-19)

In 1937 the 122 mm Model 1931 field gun barrel was mounted onto the carriage of the 152 mm Gun-howitzer Model 1937, and in this form became the 122-31/37 or A-19. This version was almost identical in appearance to the earlier gun except that the equilibriators on either side of the barrel now sloped to the rear rather than forward as they did on the Model 1931. The Germans used this version as the 12.2 cm K 390/2(r), and again incorporated them into the Atlantic Wall defences. A mobile version of this gun, the A-19S, was mounted on the SU-122 assault gun chassis.

DATA
As for Model 1931 except for the following:
WEIGHT TRAVELLING 7907 kg 17,435 lb
WEIGHT IN ACTION 7117 kg 15,693 lb
ELEVATION —2° to 65°
TRAVERSE 58°
MAXIMUM RANGE 20,400 m 22,318 yards
Self-propelled Carriage
SU-122 (KV heavy tank chassis)

122 mm Field Howitzer Model 1910/30

DATA
CALIBRE 121.92 mm 4.8 in
LENGTH OF PIECE (L/12.8) 1561.6 mm
  61.488 in
LENGTH OF RIFLING (L/9.3) 1140 mm
  44.88 in
WEIGHT TRAVELLING WITH TRAILER 2530 kg
  5579 lb
WEIGHT IN ACTION 1466 kg 3232 lb
ELEVATION —3° to 43°
TRAVERSE 4° 41'
M.V. 364 m/s 1194 ft/sec
MAXIMUM RANGE 8940 m 9780 yards
SHELL WEIGHT 21.76 kg 47.98 lb

The Russian 122 mm Field Howitzer Model 1910/30 had its origins in the Model 1910 or 10S which was a Schneider import bought in large numbers before World War 1. In 1930 The Russian artillery renovation programme involved the large numbers of 10S pieces still in service and as a result the renovated piece became the Model 1910/30 or 122-10/30. In 1941 there were still large numbers of this howitzer in service despite the fact that they were past their best days and the carriage had not been altered for modern tractors—the 122-10/30 could be towed by tractor but the original wooden-spoked wheels were still fitted and speeds were thus low. During 1941 and 1942 large numbers of this piece fell into German hands. The Germans appreciated its sturdy construction and took large numbers into their Wehrmacht inventory as the 12.2 cm leFH 388(r). A number of these found their way into Finnish Army service.

122 mm Field Howitzer Model 1938

DATA
CALIBRE 121.92 mm 4.8 in
LENGTH OF PIECE (L/22.7) 2800 mm
  110.25 in
LENGTH OF BARREL 2668 mm 105 in
LENGTH OF RIFLING (L/18.7) 2263 mm
  89.1 in
WEIGHT TRAVELLING 2800 kg 6174 lb
WEIGHT IN ACTION 2450 kg 5402 lb
ELEVATION —3° to 63° 30'
TRAVERSE (trails open) 49°
TRAVERSE (trails closed) 1° 30'
M.V. 515 m/s 1690 ft/sec
MAXIMUM RANGE 11,800 m 12,909 yards
SHELL WEIGHT 21.76 kg 47.98 lb
Self-propelled Carriages
SU-122 (T-34 tank chassis)

The 122 mm Model 1938 field howitzer was one of the most successful Russian artillery pieces produced during World War 2, and as a measure of its success it is still in widespread service in 1975. It was introduced into Russian use in late 1938 and thereafter remained as the 'standard' divisional and Army heavy howitzer throughout the war. It was a conventional, rather light design, which like most Russian weapons was reliable and sturdy. Production continued throughout the conflict, partly to meet ever increasing demands, and partly to replace the large numbers of this piece lost to the Germans in 1941 and 1942. The Germans greatly appreciated this howitzer and used it in some numbers as the 12.2 cm sFH 396(r), both as a field weapon and coastal defence weapon. Some Model 1938 howitzers found their way into service with the Finnish Army where it was (and still is) known as the m/38.

122 mm Field Howitzer Model 1938

152 mm Field Gun Model 1910/30

In the late 1930s the age of most of the pieces available to the Russian artillery arm was becoming an embarrassment to their owners and a new range of weapons was designed and developed. As it would be some time before these new weapons would be ready it was decided to update existing weapons where possible, and the elderly Model 1910 field gun was one model selected for modernisation. Originally this gun was a Schneider design licence-built in Russia. During the modernisation the carriage was extensively redesigned but remained a two-part load for towing over long distances. The barrels were re-lined and fitted with muzzle brakes, while many other detail design changes were made. The result was a virtually new gun known as the 152-10/30, and it was produced with two possible carriages—one for horse traction and another suitable for tractor towing. In 1941 and 1942 large numbers of the 152-10/30 passed into German use as the 15.2 cm K 438(r).

DATA (tractor version)
CALIBRE 152.4 mm 6 in
LENGTH OF PIECE with m.b. (L/32)
  4855 mm 191.16 in
LENGTH OF BARREL 4260 mm 167.7 in
LENGTH OF RIFLING 3304 mm 130.1 in
WEIGHT IN ACTION 6700 kg 14.773 lb

ELEVATION —7° to 37°
TRAVERSE 4° 30'
M.V. 650 m/s 2133 ft/sec
MAXIMUM RANGE 16,800 m 18,380 yards
SHELL WEIGHT 43.56 kg 96.05 lb

1. *152 mm Field Gun Model 1910/30* **2.** *152-10/30 carriage* **3.** *152-10/30 barrel on transport trailer*

1

2

3

152 mm Field Gun Model 1935 (BR-2)

DATA
CALIBRE 152.4 mm 6 in
LENGTH OF PIECE (L/50) 7620 mm 300 in
LENGTH OF BORE 6992 mm 275.27 in
WEIGHT IN ACTION 18,202 kg 40,093 lb
ELEVATION 0° to 60°
TRAVERSE 8°
M.V. 880 m/s 2887 ft/sec
MAXIMUM RANGE 27,000 m 29,540 yards
SHELL WEIGHT 48.58 kg 107 lb

The 152 mm Field Gun Model 1935, or 152-55, is one of the most obscure of all the Russian heavy guns and it is difficult to unearth any reliable information on this weapon. It was first seen in 1935 and it was apparently intended to be a long range counter-battery weapon. It was one of the small group of Russian guns that used a tractor-type suspension in place of the more conventional wheels but it was the only one of the group to use split trails. The Model 1935 does not appear to have been built in large numbers. In German recognition handbooks it is listed as the 15.2 cm K 440(r) but there are no records of any being used by German units and this may be significant.

1,2. *152 mm Field Gun Model 1935* **3,4.**
152 mm Gun-Howitzer model 1910/34r

3

1

2

152 mm Gun-Howitzer Model 1910/34r

The gun known to the Russians as the 152-10/34 was an unusual hybrid formed by the placing of the barrel of the 152 mm Howitzer Model 1937 onto the carriage of the 122 mm Field Gun Model 1931. It was produced as a stop-gap method of producing large numbers of relatively modern pieces into service quickly in the mid-1930s. The result was used as a gun-howitzer with divisional and Army artillery formations and was used in some numbers in 1941 and 1942. Before that it was used in the Winter War against Finland in 1939-1940 when some passed into Finnish service as the m/34. As usual, the Germans took numbers into service as the 15.2 cm K 433/2(r).

DATA
CALIBRE 152.4 mm 6 in
LENGTH OF PIECE (L/29) 4404 mm 173.4 in
LENGTH WITH MUZZLE BRAKE 4922 mm
193.8 in
LENGTH OF RIFLING (L/22.5) 3464 mm
136.4 in
WEIGHT TRAVELLING 7820 kg 17,243lb

WEIGHT IN ACTION 7100 kg 15,655 lb
ELEVATION —4° to 45°
TRAVERSE 58°
M.V. 650 m/s 2133 ft/sec
MAXIMUM RANGE 17,600 m 19,254 yards
SHELL WEIGHT 43.56 kg 96.05 lb

152 mm Gun-Howitzer Model 1937 (ML-20)

The Model 1937 Gun-howitzer was one of the most important of all the Russian counter-battery weapons used during World War 2. Like most Russian guns it was a hybrid using the barrel used on the 152 mm Gun-howitzer Model 1910/34r on the carriage of the 122 mm Field Gun Model 1931/37. It was produced in huge numbers and was used widely. One version, the Model 1937/43(ML-20S) was mounted on the SU-152 and JSU-152 assault guns. As an artillery piece, two differing carriages were produced. One used spoked wheels for horse traction, and the other used double-tyred steel wheels for tractor towing. In either version it was towed in one load. The Model 1937 was such an important and efficient weapon that it is still in widespread use in many armies in 1975, and in 1941 the Germans were sufficiently impressed to take into their own use any they could capture. They used them widely as the 15.2 cm KH 433/1(r), and many were incorporated into coastal defences. In Russian service the Model 1937 was known as the 152-37, and like all other Russian guns it was often called upon to act as an anti-tank gun. In this role it relied on its heavy shot weight rather than high muzzle velocity.

DATA
CALIBRE   152.4 mm   6 in
LENGTH OF PIECE (L/29)   4404 mm   173.4 in
LENGTH WITH MUZZLE BRAKE   4925 mm   193.9 in
LENGTH OF RIFLING   3467 mm   136.5 in
WEIGHT TRAVELLING   7930 kg   17,485 lb
WEIGHT IN ACTION   7128 kg   15,717 lb
ELEVATION   —2° to 65°
TRAVERSE   58°
M.V. (HE)   655 m/s   2150 ft/sec
MAXIMUM RANGE   17,265 m   18,888 yards
SHELL WEIGHT (HE)   43.56 kg   96.05 lb
Self-propelled Carriages
SU-152 (KV tank chassis)
JSU-152 (JS tank chassis)

15.2 cm KH 433/1(r) emplaced for coastal defence

152 mm Field Howitzer Model 09/30

One of the most elderly of the existing Russian guns scheduled for modernisation pending new designs expected during the 1930s was the Model 1909 howitzer. This was originally a Putilov design which saw extensive service during World War 1. During the modernisation programme the barrels were reconditioned, the carriages remained virtually unchanged, and more modern fire control equipment was incorporated. By Russian standards relatively few of these pieces were modernised and by 1941 when the German invasion took place, most appear to have been in use with second-line and training units. Some of these fell into German hands and were used by them as the 15.2 cm sFH 445(r), mainly as coastal defence weapons. In 1939 a small number of the original Model 1909 howitzers were in use with the Finnish Army. With the Russians, the modernised howitzer was known as the 152-09/30.

DATA
CALIBRE   152.4 mm   6 in
LENGTH OF PIECE (L/14.2)   2160 mm   85 in
LENGTH OF BARREL   1995 mm   78.55 in
LENGTH OF RIFLING   1657 mm   65.24 in
WEIGHT TRAVELLING   3050 kg   6725 lb
WEIGHT IN ACTION   2725 kg   6008 lb
ELEVATION   0° to 41°
TRAVERSE   5° 40'
M.V.   391 m/s   1283 ft/sec
MAXIMUM RANGE   9854 m   10,780 yards
SHELL WEIGHT   40 kg   88.2 lb

152 mm Field Howitzer Model 09/30

152 mm Field Howitzer Model 1910/30

DATA

CALIBRE 152.4 mm 6 in
LENGTH OF PIECE (L/12) 1830 mm 72 in
LENGTH OF BARREL 1672.8 mm 65.86 in
LENGTH OF RIFLING 1354.8 mm 53.34 in
WEIGHT TRAVELLING 3230 kg 7122 lb
WEIGHT IN ACTION 2580 kg 5689 lb
ELEVATION —6° 40′ to 39° 45′
TRAVERSE 4° 50′
M.V. 391 m/s 1283 ft/sec
MAXIMUM RANGE 9854 m 10,780 yards
SHELL WEIGHT 40 kg 88.2 kg
Self-propelled Carriages
SU-5-2 (T-27 tank chassis—project)
SU-6 (T-28 tank chassis)

The model 1910 howitzer was originally a French Schneider product exported to the Russian Army before World War 1—some of these eventually found their way to Finland as well. In the modernisation of the early 1930s this elderly piece was selected for updating and numerous changes were made to the gun and carriage—especially the latter which was fitted with rubber-tyred wheels for tractor towing. On the road, the revised design, now known as the 152-10/30, as towed was one load by using a two-wheeled limber under the trail spades. Like so many weapons of this early 1930s generation, the Model 1910/30 was still in use in 1941 but mainly with second-line formations. Any the Germans captured were given the designation 15.2 cm sFH 446(r) but no records can be found of any being used by them.

152 mm Field Howitzer Model 1938r (M-10)

One of the last of the planned artillery re-equipment programme to actually enter service was the Model 1938 field howitzer which entered service in late 1938 as the 152-38. This piece soon became one of the most important weapons in the heavy Russian artillery formations, and it soon proved itself to be a very successful howitzer. The sturdy carriage was designed from the outset for mechanical traction and the trails were supported on a two-wheeled axle when travelling. This carriage was also used by the 107 mm Field Gun Model 1940. Like most Russian artillery, the Model 1938 (often referred to as the M-10) was expected to be used as an anti-tank weapon and for this purpose fired a 40 kg shot (88.2 lb). After 1941 the Germans used large numbers of captured Model 1938s as the 15.2 cm sFH 443(r).

DATA
CALIBRE   152.4 mm   6 in
LENGTH OF PIECE (L/24.3) 3700 mm 145.69 in
LENGTH OF BARREL   3528 mm   138.9 in
LENGTH OF RIFLING (L/20.47)   3120 mm 122.85 in
WEIGHT TRAVELLING   4550 kg   10,033 lb
WEIGHT IN ACTION   4150 kg   9150 lb
ELEVATION   −1° to 65°
TRAVERSE   50°
M.V. (AP)   508 m/s   1667 ft/sec
M.V. (HE)   432 m/s   952 ft/sec
MAXIMUM RANGE   12,400 m   13,565 yards
SHELL WEIGHT (HE)   51.5 kg   112.6 lb

152 mm Field Howitzer Model 1943 (D-1)

In 1932 a new 152 mm howitzer was produced in Russia, and as was so often the case, this new piece was placed on an existing carriage. In this instance the carriage was that used by the readily-available 122 mm Field Howitzer Model 1938, and the new combination then became the 152 mm Field Howitzer Model 1943, or D-1. The new piece was recognisable by its large double-baffle muzzle brake. It was gradually introduced into service as the war went on but it never entirely supplanted existing models and in 1975 it remains in use in some Soviet Bloc states.

DATA
CALIBRE   152.4 mm   6 in
LENGTH OF PIECE (L/24.6)   3749 mm 147.6 in
LENGTH WITH MUZZLE BRAKE   4207 mm 165.65 in
WEIGHT TRAVELLING   3635 kg   8008 lb
WEIGHT IN ACTION   3601 kg   7940 lb
ELEVATION   −3° to +63° 30′
TRAVERSE   35°
M.V.   508 m/s   1667 ft/sec
MAXIMUM RANGE   12,400 m   13,565 yards
SHELL WEIGHT   (HE)   51.1 kg   112.6 lb

203 mm Howitzer Model 1931 (B-4)

The large 203 mm Howitzer Model 1931 was an unusual weapon in many ways, not the least of which was the use of a tracked tractor suspension in place of the more usual wheel-and-axle arrangement. Another unusual feature was the number of variants of this piece that were built, all under the basic Model 1931 designation. No fewer than six separate variants have been found, but the normal Russian designation system does not appear to differentiate between them. Some Western references refer to later variants as the Model 1935 but Russian sources use only the designation Model 1931 or 1931r. The six variants all had one thing in common and that was that the piece travelled in two loads. The variations differed in the type of barrel carriage and the method of suspension used. The first five variants used a variety of differing wheel sizes and the latest variant used a tracked barrel carriage. Another change was that the first three versions used an L/22 barrel and for the last three versions this was lengthened to L/25. The ammunition remained the same for all the six versions except the first which was slightly lighter. The latest variant appears to have been produced in 1937. As with so many other Russian guns after 1941, the various versions of the Model 1931 entered German service. In typically thorough German fashion the six variants were given German designations and in the absence of reliable Russian information regarding designations the German designations have been used in the data tables. As far as can be ascertained the German designations were given in chronological order and the first version was known as the 20.3 cm H 503(r). The later versions carried the prefix of /1, /2, /3, /4 and /5(r). Only the /3, /4 and /5 versions, all with L/25 barrels, were pressed into German service and it can be assumed that not many of the earlier L/22 versions were captured, doubtless due to a Russian retrofitting programme. The captured howitzers appear to have been used on the Eastern Front only and very few were captured by the Allies elsewhere.

Data

GERMAN DESIGNATION	20.3 cm H 503(r)	20.3 cm H 503/1 (r)	20.3 cm H 503/2(r)
CALIBRE	203.2 mm/8 in	203.2 mm/8 in	203.2 mm/8 in
LENGTH OF PIECE (L/22)	4466 mm/175.85 in	4466 mm/175.85 in	4466 mm/175.85 in
LENGTH OF BARREL	4294 mm/169 in	4294 mm/169 in	4294 mm/169 in
LENGTH OF RIFLING	3360.6 mm/132.32 in	3360.6 mm/132.32 in	3360.6 mm/132.32 in
WEIGHT IN ACTION	15796 kg/34830 lb	15800 kg/34840 lb	15800 kg/34840 lb
ELEVATION	0° to +60°	0° to +60°	0° to +60°
TRAVERSE	8°	8°	8°
M.V.	538 m/s//1765 ft/sec	550 m/s//1805 ft/sec	550 m/s//1805 ft/sec
MAXIMUM RANGE	12800 m/14000 yards	16000 m/17504 yards	16000 m/17504 yards
SHELL WEIGHT	98 kg/216.1 lb	100 kg/220.5 lb	100 kg/220.5 lb
	First version	Same carriage as /3	Same carriage as /4
		Barrel carriage as /3	Barrel carriage as /4
		Large barrel carriage wheels	Small barrel carriage wheels

GERMAN DESIGNATION	20.3 cm H 503/3(r)	20.3 cm H 503/4(r)	20.3 cm H 503/5(r)
CALIBRE	203.2 mm/8 in	203.2 mm/8 in	203.2 mm/8 in
LENGTH OF PIECE (L/25)	5087 mm/200.3 in	5087 mm/200.3 in	5087 mm/200.3 in
LENGTH OF BARREL	4915 mm/193.53 in	4915 mm/193.53 in	4915 mm/193.53 in
LENGTH OF RIFLING	3981 mm/156.75 in	3981 mm/156.75 in	3981 mm/156.75 in
WEIGHT IN ACTION	17700 kg/39029 lb	17700 kg/39029 lb.	17700 kg/39029 lb
ELEVATION	0° to +60°	0° to +60°	0° to +60°
TRAVERSE	8°	8°	8°
M.V.	607 m/s//1992 ft/sec	607 m/s//1992 ft/sec	607 m/s//1992 ft/sec
SHELL WEIGHT	100 kg/220.5 lb	100 kg/220.5 lb	100 kg/220.5 lb
	Same carriage as /1	Same carriage as /2	Same carriage as /4
	Barrel carriage as /1	Barrel carriage as /2	Tracked barrel carriage
	Large barrel carriage wheels	Small barrel carriage wheels	

203 mm Howitzer Model 1931—L/22 version

203 mm Howitzer Model 1931